CLOSURES

GRACE LAVERY

CLOS

URES

HETEROSEXUALITY AND THE AMERICAN SITCOM

DUKE UNIVERSITY PRESS   DURHAM AND LONDON   2024

© 2024 DUKE UNIVERSITY PRESS
All rights reserved
Printed and bound by CPI Group (UK) Ltd, Croydon, CR0 4YY
Project Editor: Ihsan Taylor
Designed by Matthew Tauch
Typeset in Portrait Text and Unbounded by Copperline
Book Services

Library of Congress Cataloging-in-Publication Data
Names: Lavery, Grace E., author.
Title: Closures : heterosexuality and the American sitcom /
Grace Lavery.
Description: Durham : Duke University Press, 2024. | Includes
bibliographical references and index. | Contents: Full House—
Friends—Parallels.
Identifiers: LCCN 2023026657 (print)
LCCN 2023026658 (ebook)
ISBN 9781478030140 (paperback)
ISBN 9781478025894 (hardcover)
ISBN 9781478059134 (ebook)
Subjects: LCSH: Situation comedies (Television programs)—United States—
History and criticism. | Situation comedies (Television programs)—
Social aspects—United States. | Sex role on television. | Heterosexuality. |
Homosexuality on television. | BISAC: PERFORMING ARTS / Television /
History & Criticism | SOCIAL SCIENCE / Gender Studies
Classification: LCC PN1992.8.C66 L384 2024 (print) |
LCC PN1992.8.C66 (ebook) | DDC 791.45/6170973—dc23/eng/20230913
LC record available at https://lccn.loc.gov/2023026657
LC ebook record available at https://lccn.loc.gov/2023026658

Cover art: Ed O'Neill and Katey Sagal, *Married . . . with Children*
publicity photo. Fox/Photofest © Fox Broadcasting Company.

CONTENTS

FORMULA

The short book that follows constitutes either a long essay or a series of very short fragments concerning the American sitcom, as it
was instantiated between, roughly, World War II and the COVID-19
pandemic that began in 2019. Those dates are not accidental. The
sitcom developed to suit the consumer interests of the expanding
audience of baby boomers and their parents, in the era during which
television ownership became a common aspect of American domestic life: in 1950, 9 percent of American households owned a television; by 1978, it was 98 percent. In 2011, the percentage fell to 96.7
percent.[1] That dip reflected an increasing reliance on personal com-
puters to consume media, although the Nielsen company, which
specializes in collating consumer information on television, now
includes broadband-enabled "smart TVs" among the devices that
it counts as televisions for the sake of its data gathering—which
means that the proportion of viewers who watch new shows when
they are first broadcast is likely much lower. While some sitcoms
are still made, and even watched, it nonetheless makes sense to refer to the genre in the past tense for structural reasons: First, because the displacement of television services onto online platforms
like Netflix, which usually release multiple episodes of a show at
once, has dispensed with the conventional serialization devices
that structured many of the sitcom's signal formal properties. Second, because many of those formal properties had been dispensed
with even before the migration into digital media, and while it is
possible to imagine a sitcom (indeed, there are many) without a
laugh track, a soundstage, or a strong form of episodic narrative

closure, the loss of all three (to the cringe, the "single camera" green screen set, and the seasonal arc, respectively) has created, over the past few decades, a set of post-sitcom genres with sitcom elements: the dramedy (*Ally McBeal, Sex and the City*), the comedy mystery (*Search Party, Only Murders in the Building*), the comedy procedural (*House, M.D.; Murderville*), and plenty more. Nonetheless, allowing the sitcom slightly more than three score years and ten, between the broadcast of the first episode of *Mary Kay and Johnny* on the DuMont Television Network on November 18, 1947, and the final episodes of *BoJack Horseman* bundled out by Netflix on January 31, 2020 (just before the lockdowns began in the United States), the genre effectuated a complex, subtle, and arguably unrivaled-in-scale change in American attitudes and therefore in the attitudes of those around the world whose lives were touched by American empire and the American culture industry, concerning love, sex, family, plot, work, race, and identity.

Justifiably notorious for its formulae, the sitcom is better defined from the middle out than deductively; this book as a whole constitutes a definition of the term. But I take the three salient variables to be (1) a laugh track—that is, either recordings of a live studio audience, a "canned" recording, or (almost ubiquitously) a combination of the two; (2) a soundstage set that remains consistent over time, whether Mary Tyler Moore's Minneapolis pied-à-terre or Monica Gellar's massive West Village pad; and (3) a strong form of episodic modularity that produces comic closure at the scale of the episode rather than the yearlong season or the whole series. And again, while it is possible to imagine a sitcom that has *only* a laugh track but neither of the others (like the British show *I'm Alan Partridge*), *only* a soundstage but neither of the others (though I've failed to think of a show that fits this description but isn't a soap opera), or a strong form of episodic closure but neither of the others (like *Family Guy*), a show with *none* of them would not be a sitcom.

Of these three elements, this book is most directly concerned with the third. My book title, *Closures*, is designed to highlight the paradoxical quality of a comedy—that is, a narrative of social harmonization through the world-founding creation of a family—which must repeat its peculiar *form* of comic closure again and again, week after week, for as long as the ruse can be sustained. So, despite its reputation as a normative model of heterosexual social reproduction, the sitcom in fact presents the heterosexual family neither as the inevitable point of departure for comic plot nor indeed its point of arrival. Whereas in a Shakespearean comedy like *A Midsummer Night's Dream,* say, the aftermath of a wedding could no more be depicted than could life after death, the sitcom dwells in the present continuous, where family is always on the verge of disintegrating and always in the process of being repaired or reconstituted. Procedural television shows, from medical dramas to whodunnits, depend on strong forms of closure at the scale of the episode too, but unlike sitcoms they are structured around *cases*: new characters and settings introduced in each episode to host the main cast and who leave only minimal traces, if any, behind after the diagnosis has been determined, culprit identified, or verdict returned. Sitcoms require narrative closure and ideally the establishment of whatever dynamic homeostasis prevailed at the episode's start, but without a case of any kind to solve, they must design social settings—whether of family, friends, or the workplace—capable of sustaining not a singular closure but closures, plural.

The models of comic subjectivity and character that emerge from this metadiegetic necessity are original and distinct to the sitcom: with the passing of the sitcom, so passes the age of Morticia Addams, Mork, Sally Solomon, Dwight Schrute, and all the many other sitcom characters upon whom the imposition of heterosexual relations generated powerfully contrarian practices of anti-familial eccentricity. The practice of sex and gender under the aegis of the *situation* has produced characters like these not merely appealing to transsexuals (by common but sadly uncitable observance, trans people seem to watch a lot of sitcoms) but structurally transsexual in their very position, constantly foreclosed in their asymptotic but nonetheless extravagant attempts to wrangle being from becoming.

Three quick notes about method: First, I want to be clear that the readings in the sitcom that follow are *literary* readings, which is to say that they seek to animate the interpretive questions raised by this most flimsy, and in some ways most abject, of genres. I focus on individual episodes of long-running shows and therefore call on small visual or textual details to yield evidence about the nature of the genre as a whole. Since the formulaic quality of the sitcom is something of a given, both for this study and in general, often what might seem like a detail about a given show might be treated as a trope common to the genre. For example, in a certain episode of *Sister, Sister*, Tia and Tamera Mowry are sent home with eggs that they are to protect as though they were babies. Of course the "egg sitting" trope is not uncommon in US sex education classes, and it is also remarkably common in sitcoms and associated media set in high schools: the website TV Tropes collects forty-one instances of "egg sitting" in live-action television yet doesn't include the episode of *Sister, Sister*.[2] Parts, but not all, of whatever one could say about the egg in *Sister, Sister* could also be said about Niles taking care of a bag of flour in *Frasier*, Chris being given a brown egg by a racist teacher in *Everybody Hates Chris*, Kelso fraudulently obtaining a second egg in *That '70s Show*, and so on. For these reasons, my argument progresses according to its own internal logic rather than according to the chronological history of the genre, to which I make occasional reference but rarely accord any particular explanatory power. If indeed the sitcom is an especially formulaic genre, then it is thereby also an especially *anachronistic* genre, in which an individual joke ("we finish each other's . . ." // "sandwiches?") could belong to its historical moment but could just as easily be a remnant of a past moment ("[the Chinese] just call it food") or even a prefiguration of a moment still to come.

Yet the converse is equally true: even the most hackneyed of tropes may be subtly undone in the instantiation, and it may be that the very application of a cliché itself entails its dialectical reversal. My goal here is to encourage the perversities of the sitcom to endure into the critical scene; I seek neither to elevate individual works out of the generic morass ("generic" being no discredit to a work of art), nor to account for the genre as if it were a singular twitch of capital—a culture industry to be loved and loathed on the basis of its hegemonic grip on the world. The sitcom is interesting because of its unfinishedness—and perhaps because of the unfinishedness it exposes in the general project of heterosexual social reproduction. I have no interest in evaluating any of the objects I discuss here, on either aesthetic or political grounds; genre studies like this are justified if they can account for the cultural problematics that a given genre formulates and sustains. Few genres, and certainly not the sitcom, determine the political content with which they are instantiated in a given instance: over the course of this book, I engage sitcoms whose political commitments range from crypto fascist, through mildly conservative, to liberally feminist, to radically emancipatory, and so on. I've also found it useful while teaching the sitcom to be clear—though surely nobody who has read this far can be under any illusions on this point!—that I can't supply any advice to the prospective television showrunner. I have no practical experience working in this particular sector of the culture industry, and I am not interested in acquiring any.

Second, this book *is* committed, albeit in a rather half-articulated and gun-shy way, to the program of family abolition articulated by Charles Fourier and those feminist and abolitionist writers who have written on the topic since: from Alexandra Kollontai and Shulamith Firestone to Lola Olufemi and Sophie Lewis. An extended essay on the formal properties of the sitcom is not the place to rehearse the case for family abolition (rather than reform, or anti-homophobic "love makes a family" activism, etc.), but suffice it to say that when I describe "the family" as it is depicted in the sitcom, I am describing a set of social relations that are reproduced against the interests of every individual bound by them—including those of the patriarch, though his least of all—and which are felt as suffering and compulsion whenever they are felt at all. I suspect it goes without saying that these coercions are mitigated not one iota when, as in *Modern Family* or *The New Normal*, the parents in question are homosexual men.

The term *heterosexual* is used here to describe not an orientation but an exertion of power. Indeed, I am generally skeptical of "sexual orientation" as a model of erotic object choice, for reasons long established in queer studies: perhaps it could be true, for some fraction of people, that erotic objects tend to (1) belong to the same group, (2) be primarily defined by sex (rather than hair color, personality, etc.), and (3) remain consistent over time. But even if such a group exists, and we have ample reason to be skeptical of the notion, it wouldn't necessarily follow that it possessed what we usually call a "sexual orientation," unless we could *also* establish that these erotic object choices were predictable in advance rather than collated inductively after the fact. Sigmund Freud's theory of sexuality as reaction formation strikes me as more persuasive: that more important to a person than their erotic object choices is their erotic *aversions*, and that "sexual orientation" designates simply what is left of polymorphous perversity after shame, disgust, and fear have done their work. Heterosexuality, however, unquestionably exists as an organ of power. Psychically, it functions to repudiate or disavow any possibility of identity with an erotic object: a man, penetrating a woman, is experiencing heterosexuality in so far as the act of penetration affirms for him his essential difference from the body he is penetrating. Politically, it works to instill the family as the basic unit of socialization, to move women into unwaged reproductive work, and to self-replicate through the reaction formations already mentioned—shame, fear, and disgust. The lesbian feminist Sheila Jeffreys, who is of course well known for her critiques of queer politics, kink, and porn and for her disdain of trans women in particular, nonetheless developed a useful analysis of heterosexuality as "the sexuality of male supremacy which eroticizes inequality."[3] While I acknowledge the debt of this work to lesbian feminists like Gloria Anzaldúa, Cherríe Moraga, Adrienne Rich, and Monique Wittig, I don't use the phrase "compulsory heterosexuality" because I consider it pleonastic: heterosexuality simply names the compulsory sexual disconnection that patriarchy requires in order to organize the social field in the interests of men and of capital. I consider this work a feminist work of scholarship, dedicated to the illumination and extirpation of patriarchal social forms; I am, certainly, committed to the trans feminism articulated by Emma Heaney and Jules Gill-Peterson, among others, and this work has been shaped by reading the work of social reproduction theorists and Marxist feminists like Amy De'Ath and Kay Gabriel. It is not, however, a theoretical intervention in itself, much less a political one, but a formal assessment of a genre.

Third, to refer to "the sitcom" as though it named an archive that a person could claim to have mastered is to invite trouble. I have lost track of the number of times that a colleague or friend, upon hearing I've been writing a book about sitcoms, asks me what I make of *some particular show they love*, which I've never heard of, and which, were I to try to watch it with anything like the rigor required to do the job properly, would insert another three months, at least, into my research schedule. So, hands up: I haven't watched every American sitcom, and I don't believe anyone could (or, frankly, should). I haven't even watched every *episode* of every show I mention here, though I've watched all the episodes of the shows I discuss in any detail. This book, like the sitcom itself, aims for something between coverage and exemplarity: a lot of items are covered quickly in passing, and a fairly high degree of exposure to the genre is assumed, but only a smaller number of shows are treated in depth. A different book, with different claims, could be written focused only on the shows I've declined to talk about in detail: *M*A*S*H*, *Seinfeld*, *The Golden Girls*, *Parks and Recreation*, and so on. I've tended to pass over shows whose reception has already been, more or less, on the money: I have little to add to Sianne Ngai's exquisite rendering of *I Love Lucy*, for example, but want to give *The Brady Bunch* its long-overdue desert.[4] I've tried to think about the question of exemplarity as I would if I were writing a book about Victorian novels: no reader would expect me to have read them *all*, yet somewhere between the main five Charles Dickens novels and *Middlemarch* and the twenty-five thousand or so entries in what Margaret Cohen and Franco Moretti have called "the great unread," there's a threshold for credibility. Negotiating that threshold has engendered a peculiar critical device, which I didn't anticipate deploying when I began work on this project. When there isn't a particular reason to do otherwise, which in about half the cases here there is, I have defaulted to writing about *pilot episodes*. This plan carried the risk of skewing my analysis to emphasize properties particular to pilot episodes, especially the more-than-usually-schematic framing of both *the situation* and its incompleteness to which pilot episodes, naturally enough, are prone. I hope I've offset that risk in the study itself. But this device has two justifications: it has helped me clarify ways in which a given show's *situation* is, indeed, often the fundamental subject of my analysis; and I hope that it will help readers for whom a given show is new catch up at least to this book, if not to the show itself, by watching a single episode rather than (so to speak) opening an unread book at a chapter somewhere in the middle, or else reading from the start.

I'm thankful to my friends, colleagues, lovers, puppies, and comrades, who have taken me outside many a situation, and without whom work would be unthinkable and writing unwritable. I'm grateful to the students and assistant teachers who took part in the two lecture courses on the sitcom that I have taught, and to Cheng-Chai Chiang and Shirl Yang, who organized a seminar on "Awkwardness" at which I presented the section of this book concerned with Urkel. I am grateful to two anonymous reviewers at Duke University Press and to this book's editor, Elizabeth Ault, who helped tighten—but also loosen—this rather retentive manuscript. I am grateful to Hannah Zeavin, who commissioned part of this work for *Parapraxis* and whose conversation and engagement have shaped much of my thinking on these topics. And I'm thankful to Susan Stryker, who has encouraged me in this work and in much besides. I dedicate this book to the city of Brooklyn, New York, where it was written, and where the burdens of protagonism are nobody's to bear alone.

PART 1
FULL HOUSE

— What are you staring at, Monsieur Max?

— The celluloid of your legs.

— What a fool you are: they're made of broken glass!

The entire piquancy of this anecdote lies in the finesse of her repartee.

MICHEL LEIRIS, *Nights as Day, Days as Night*

Altogether

To begin with, then: the family. But even before we begin, we confront a certain challenge, which is that in comedies, the family is either a point of embarkation or a destination. It is definitively both, in fact: if comedy is comic, it is so only because it establishes continuity between the love (et al.) that one takes, and the love (et al.) that one makes. The suspicion that what we call love might turn out to have been nothing more than the holding pattern of a plane that never lands, a self-reproducing ideological matrix, that love might involve neither takeoff nor landing, that it is merely an endless, autotelic *situation*—this is the fantasy that is formalized in our ambivalent fear and desire for *the sitcom*. The situation comedy may therefore be uniquely badly designated, but the genre has always known the fact, and since its earliest instantiations it has set up little dioramas, indexing but (supposedly) declining to depict the situation comedy as a nightmarish and eternal recurrence. A book could be written—in fact, several have been—about the sitcom as it ambivalently longs to have been, about the shows within shows: about *Horsin' Around*, *WandaVision*, *Terrance and Phillip*, *When the Whistle Blows*, *The Alan Brady Show*, *Pucks!*, *Father Ben*, and so on. Critics of the sitcom have long noted the inadequacy of the sitcom-as-realism position: Lynn Spigel writes that "early sitcoms typically depicted the family as a theater troupe rather than as a 'real' family."[1] But the very fact that these meta-shows are themselves meta-clichés tells us that the sitcom never finalized the condition of glorious homeostasis, any more than heterosexuality did, and that a cunning enough Truman Burbank could even find, hidden among the catchphrases, threats, and little white lies, instructions on how to escape.

Heterosexuality affords an intimately scaled model of exogamy, since while, importantly, any body is capable of sustaining penetration, only the heterosexual body treats the introduction of an external element as the imposition of a difference. In a heterosexual system, penetration marks the introduction of an element that must be *handled*—the discourse called "sexual ethics" being only the most spectacularly coercive method of evacuation. Pregnancy is another, if it is not the first: by capturing and nurturing the invasive element, the gestational body converts difference into sameness, finally enabling the full objectification of that difference in the form of an abstract person, a baby. The idea that giving birth therefore blends the functions of excretion and castration reformulates one aspect of Freud's occasionally rather outlandish claims in "Femininity"—baby as phallus, birth as castration, nursing as re-suturing.[2] Whether the sitcom system is implicitly or explicitly a heterosexual system depends, to some extent, on its treatment of the external element: the neighbor, the Urkel; the nuisance, the

Soup Nazi; or else the specially engrafted sex partner—the Janice, say. Janice isn't a perfect example, because although her bleat initially marks her out as merely one annoyance in a series of sexual dysfunctions, *Friends* seems, eventually, to notice that she has been asked to carry much more than her fair share of the show's intensely aversive feelings about female pleasure, which endows her, albeit belatedly, with some kind of pathos by way of compensation.

We call generic any system that converts difference into sameness: the gestational body, from a certain angle, might therefore found a genre—where once there was merely Homer and Marge, now there are *The Simpsons*. That show, as it happens, debuted in 1989, the same year that *Sim City* was released: both *Sim-* franchises began by proposing modestly satirical models for the white American bourgeoisie but thrived by populating their social fields with massively diversified populations, each subordinated to the same quirky figurative logics: yellow skin for whiteness; desires depicted as thought bubbles. We sense Springfield's density in the opening credits, when the camera passes from Marge and Maggie on a hill to Lisa cycling into the garage, over a massive array of dozens upon dozens of minor characters. After thirty-three years, though, they're minor no longer: each of these figures has had at least an episode dedicated to their interiority, cycled in and out of protagonism. *The Simpsons* may not even feel like a sitcom, because its methods of reproducing the homeostatic family at the scale of an episode, while brutal in their efficiency, seem to build a world laterally, fleshing in the life of a midsized town gradually but lavishly. The situation of *The Simpsons* is not exactly a situation but a full impressionist landscape.

If it is to serve as an instruction manual for exogamy, heterosexual relationality must frame-in space procedures that are usually experienced in the medium of time—hence, the term *situation* seems to designate a quasi-spatial form, even if the relations and conditions it circumscribes are more properly temporal. "Family" may indicate a home, but it may also indicate a phase. Moreover, the situation is, typically, neither inert in itself nor unreactive to other situations. The situation comedy's great secret, hiding in plain sight since long before the first television was switched on, long before *Mary Kay and Johnny* appeared in the goggle-box, is this: that everyone is more or

1.1 An assortment of *Simpsons* characters stands on a green hill topped by a smoking nuclear plant.

less the same in the sack. Sex brings people together, even as *hetero-sex* demands that people be split apart. Among the central insights of psychoanalysis is that sex is unsexing: men are castrated, women are endowed with the phallus, and vice versa, again and again, until bodies are no longer subject to the conventional divisions with which we dissociate what is yours from what is mine. Jacques Lacan's quip that there is no sexual relation remains a perspective frozen in the tragic—sex as protagonism, as *hamartia*, and ultimately as tragic nonevent.[3] The queer revamp, with its necessary and bracing defacement of the sexual pastoral, trades in sexual ethics for sexual seriousness—play itself, one suspects, sense-impressions of the thud and squelch of colliding, smelly objects, slides off the shattered, suicidal subject. The subject of anal penetration that Leo Bersani conjures may shatter, then, but he doesn't *prolapse*—nothing so lurid, so prurient, will distract us from the sublime object of ideological annihilation.[4] Sex as comedy, as situation, denudes even this subject still further: already deprived of ego, ethics, and relation, the sitcom guy finds his dignity shredded one last time, by a bathos more ruthless than even Leo Bersani.

So then, the wild oscillations of gross flesh are frozen in place by the ritual of comic convergence: epithalamion for a distended, brutalized self, stuck onto another, engrafted so that each resents whatever resources the other consumes, *situation* displacing *relation*. Here's the weird thing about sitcoms, and I'm just going to say it, here it comes: everyone thinks that sitcoms mostly depict normative nuclear families, but it isn't so. They mostly depict blended families (widows, divorcés, lodgers, roommates) cohabiting, and the stakes of that cohabitation are usually both greater and more complex than one tends to assume. *Leave It to Beaver* is less typical than *The Brady Bunch*, and even the former is less ideologically reproductive than it's cracked up to be, in the sense that the Beav's domestic orthodoxies are revisited, albeit only on the modular episodic scale, by a pipe, a neighbor, a scrape. A less frequently observed origin point, but in some senses a more plausible one, would be *The Addams Family*: famously creepy and kooky, despite the cohort's apparently shared *ookiness*, the collectivity could hardly warrant the intensifying adverb "altogether," since it derives from the arrangement of different elements, from different genres, which are unsettling (if they are) only on the basis of the convergence of incongruous types. A typical sitcom family, the only thing they have in common is that each of them has nothing in common with the others. Though *The Addams Family* debuted as a cartoon in the 1930s, it's been part of broadcast media for six decades, during which time the Addamses, in one form or another, have rarely been off the air; one feels little need to reconstruct the Chinese dictionary–like taxonomy in which "vamp mother" and "Latin lover" collided with "prim Pilgrim daughter" and "deceptively normal-looking son." But it wasn't Halloween, and it wasn't anything so straightforward as *The Munsters*: if anything, it's the sedimentary palimpsest of American degeneracy that Charles Addams had initially set out to lampoon and that emerges in the documentary genre in the camp classic *Grey Gardens*.

The pilot episode, "The Addams Family Goes to School," seems shockingly familiar from the overwrought perspective of 2022, when the question of which community norms should be formalized in the curricula of public schools has become a newly urgent one. Wednesday (Lisa Loring), whose name no less than outfit suggests a kind of Puritan pedantry, finds herself targeted by the local truant officer, Mr. Hilliard (Allyn Joslyn); a modern Puritanism asserts its claim on the state, and on the titular *Family*, in the allegori-

1.2 In a cartoon by Charles Addams, the Addams family—Uncle Fester, Pugsley, Lurch, Morticia, Gomez, and Wednesday—disembarks from a bus.

cal designation of the local principal, Miss Comstock (Madge Blake). While many or even most sitcom pilots introduce their situations by, in one way or another, erecting them, *The Addams Family* invites its viewers to discover one, along with Mr. Hilliard, through whose point of view the audience first glimpses the stately 001 Cemetery Lane, in the episode's first shot. Unlike Hilliard, we've been told what to expect: "their house is a museum," and so it is. As we wander through the set in the episode's opening scenes, we encounter, along with our jumpy avatar, a series of freaky stuffed animals, a creepy hand—Thing—in a box (a triply ungendered sexual organ, then), and other eclectic antiquities. Yet something unmistakably Hollywood has happened. The Addams cartoons, published in the *New Yorker*, depicted a collection of bridge-and-tunnel New Yorkers, but the sitcom's set could only be in California, not so much Little Edie as William Randolph Hearst.

Despite being approached by Mr. Hilliard as merely indigent old money, whose resistance to the depredations of the state requires

1.3 In the pilot episode of *The Addams Family*, Wednesday Addams leads the visiting truancy officer through the entryway of the Addams mansion. A giant stuffed bear, Victorian staircase, and mounted swordfish are all on display.

neither more nor less tact than one might deploy against any other member of the class, in fact the Addamses are a peculiarly Californian species of magpie: eclecticism not as worldly collective style but as a fraught ethics without historical origin or terminus. There will be no educating Wednesday Addams because there will be no extracting her from the ruins of history in which she has made her home; there is nothing to begin, nothing to grow.

And there is much to kill. What kind of a mother does this?

The answer is, every one. When we find Morticia (Carolyn Jones), she is snipping the bud off the rose, before it has even opened. If, as feels inevitable, we must talk about this image ("deadheading") in relation to castration, the tightness of the bud might prove something of a thorn, since it is Wednesday's future whose foreclosure Mr. Hilliard has come to redress. Yet the coziness with which Morticia completes her ministrations upon the plant heads indicates an unexpected aspect of the situation at 001 Cemetery: that clearly life will find a way to reconstruct the part that has been

1.4 As Morticia Addams, Carolyn Jones uses shears to behead a rose growing in her greenhouse in an episode of *The Addams Family*.

chopped off and will do so at a pace such that tending the flowers is a pleasant chore rather than a solace or a burden. But if Morticia feels easy deflowering her plants, her concern for Wednesday's welfare indicates that something profoundly challenges her when it comes to the role of mother, in which aspect castration remains (at least when conducted in so leisurely a manner) still generally frowned upon.

Sure, Jan

So ubiquitous has been the sitcom's reputation as formulaic dreck, even among those who enjoy it, that it has also served as a useful scapegoat for the harms engendered by social form itself, chiefly the family form. The French director François Ozon's 1998 movie *Sitcom* executes a brisk satire on the sitcom as a metonymic critique of compulsory heterosexuality as an entailment of the French

1.5 In a still from *Sitcom*, Nicolas, Sophie, and their parents sit around a dining room table.

bourgeois family. One day, Papa brings a lab rat home; the rat then proceeds to have contact with each member of the family circle in turn, precipitating the shy, bookish son to announce that he's gay and the cheerfully white-bread daughter to jump out a window and begin BDSM-inflected relationships with her boyfriend and the maid, whose husband seduces the son. Her family's disintegration intensifies Mama's commitment to holding the family together, until that very commitment causes her to seduce her son, who is now regularly hosting groups of pierced young men in his room while swishing around in tight PVC pants. The film's title, then, serves as a satirical shorthand for both the family form and the increasingly lurid methods by which it is safeguarded in the face of its disassembly, both a specific form and the (in this case, maternal) drive to form and be formalized as such.

Relatedly, we might recall the deployment of soap opera tropes in some of David Lynch's early works. In *Twin Peaks*, the recurring *Invitation to Love* soap opera sequences serve not to traduce the family form as it is replicated among the Palmers, the Hornes, and others but perversely to incorporate something from an apparently degraded model of that form—to access, through the psychoanalytically primal scene of televisual spectatorship, the naive transcendence of sentiment. These tropes also appear in *Blue Velvet*, in which a boy on the cusp of manhood is led astray from his age-appropriate romantic interest by an older woman, whose desire to be beaten and humiliated violently disrupts the boy's heterosexualization. In its place is erected a new Oedipal circuit, according to whose logic Jeffrey Beaumont (Kyle MacLachlan) adopts the role of abusive father, at the cost of submitting himself wholly to the desire of Dorothy Vallens (Isabella Rossellini). Yet in a reversal characteristic of Lynch, the satirical energy that had seemed poised to undermine the social reproduction of the biological family in favor of a kinkier new psychic configuration in fact rebounds against Dorothy herself, the very wholeness of whose desire compels her to stand in Jeffrey's domestic environment, naked and shivering, muttering "he put his disease in me," to the mutually magnetizing horror of Jeffrey and his age-appropriate belle, Sandy Williams (Laura Dern). Since Dorothy is unable to hold in her own body the desire that governs her every movement and choice, all that remains is for Jeffrey to encircle his girlfriend and exclude the desiring mother whose appearance has rendered his environment unstable. When Jeffrey delivers the line "maybe the robins are here," calling back to Sandy's sweet and prophetic dream that "there is trouble 'til the robins come," what might on paper have seemed a gormless cliché sanctifies what Bersani calls the "oval-like intimacy" and re-enchants the very heterosexual social reproduction that we had been led to believe was the object of our satire.[5] Those who argue that *Blue Velvet* exposes a *seedy underbelly* to the American family have the matter exactly wrong: Lynch's work consistently proves that the family survives through a rigorous moral hygiene, which succeeds on every level, including that of the aesthetic.

In both *Sitcom* and *Blue Velvet*, neither of which is a sitcom (I suppose they're queer farce and noir melodrama, respectively), sitcom tropes are mediated through the organizing figure of the desiring mother. In *Sitcom*, Mama's transgressive sexual designs on her son are indistinguishable from a desire for form: she is both a character and an Oedipal limit on the family members' capacity to individualize. In *Blue Velvet*, Dorothy's omnivorous mothering takes in her absented and possibly interchangeable husband and son, Don and Donnie, her abusive lover Frank, and Jeffrey; but moreover it likewise figures as the castrating edge of form itself. We might refer to this condition as the mother's uncastrated desire: whereas, in developmental psychoanalysis, the family romance depends on the fantasy of maternal castration—for any proper Oedipalization but also in particular for the fetishist, the narcissist, and the hysteric—a mother who desires cannot be Oedipalized and can only be registered as the omnivorous doppelgänger of the family as such. But Dorothy and Mama refuse to limit their mothering to the developmental care of particular minors: their maternal actions depend, rather, on thwarting and absorbing whichever objects present themselves, and combusting to fuel more laborious desiring.

On the other hand, the only possible maternal response to the problematic fact of desire is family abolition; there can be no accommodation of uncastrated maternal desire within a system not merely predicated on but ultimately identical with its negation. *Sitcom* concludes with Papa microwaving and eating the rat and then transforming into an enormous rat, filmed in extreme close-up, which attacks mother and son and is eventually killed by the rest of the now de-formed family, who all visit his grave in a short final scene. Free from patriarch and perhaps even from patriarchy, they stand together as a group of equals, survivors of the family form, before heading to the café across the way together. Whether or not one wishes to refer to *Sitcom* and *Blue Velvet* as satires, the metalepsis by which representations of maternal desire can be felt as a structuring principle of form can also be found in sitcoms that are no more conscious of the genre's reputation than they have to be.

In her 1996 essay "Lesbian Economics," the philosopher Jeffner Allen describes the "heterosexual grid" into which women are dislocated.[6] This grid spatializes and formalizes the logic of unending obligation to men, along a vertical axis that prioritizes those men "above" and "below" (for example, in the employer/employee relation) and a horizontal axis that prioritizes those men to whom one is implicitly compared (colleagues, spouses, etc.). Allen's grid constitutes a diagram to replace the "separate spheres" framework that has governed the borders of public and private, and therefore waged and unwaged labor, since the nineteenth century. The traditional sitcom set—a domestic space with a wall missing, where the world looks in—therefore presents a threshold of public and private, or perhaps more directly figures as an abscess or lesion, in which an internal regulation (of affect, etc.) that should be the proper domain of the organic unit now takes place while leaking into the surrounding cavity. "Don't wash your dirty linen in public" is as the same as saying "Don't show your shit smears to the audience." Lauren Berlant and Michael Warner offer a distinct set of spatial metaphorics by reporting, under the heading "There Is Nothing More Public Than Privacy," on various "publics" that are "organized around sex, but not necessarily sex *acts* in the usual sense."[7] Spheres, "zones," and grids are clearly present.

The opening titles of *The Brady Bunch* postdate the game show *Hollywood Squares* by three years, and clearly most of the show's initial audience would be familiar with this arrangement of faces separated into nine boxes. Yet while the *Hollywood Squares* spatialization is functional—it forms the basis of the game of tic-tac-toe in which two specific observers, the show's contestants, compete to win a Botany 500 wardrobe or other prize—there is no obvious *usefulness* implied by this image, unless it is the rather morbid usefulness for heterosexuality of the correspondence between Mom's three girls and Pop's three "men." The fairy-tale lyrics, meanwhile, suggest that indeed this is a heterosexual grid of absolute obligation, in which the three daughters are deal sweeteners for lonely Brady, three brides for three brothers:

> Here's the story of a lovely lady
> who was bringing up three very lovely girls.
> All of them had hair of gold, like their mother—
> the youngest one in curls.

> It's the story of a man named Brady
> who was busy with three boys of his own.
> They were four men, living all together,
> yet they were all alone.

Golden loveliness for the girls, manly loneliness for the boys—and of course, this is to become Brady's Bunch after all, not the lady's, whose proper name remains unsung. The parallel construction is amplified by an accomplished caesura in the third line of each verse,

1.6 In the introduction to *The Brady Bunch*, the children and their parents, all presented against a blue background, are gathered around a black square in the center.

pairing up the modifying phrases "like their mother" with "living all together"—a relationship of verisimilitude on the one hand, and of congruence on the other. Meanwhile, the hierarchization of the outer columns by age produces a neat developmental map of heterosexual becoming: Marcia and Greg—who could almost pair off—at the top, Cindy and Bobby unworn by cares at the bottom, and Jan and Peter in the middle, on the cusp of a risk.

Yet even this minimally functionalist reading already emplots too much an image whose governance is geometric, abstract, and synchronic. Unlike *Hollywood Squares*, these figures aren't inhabiting boxes in an architectural whole—rather, their dislocated faces, which of course were filmed on the same spot at different times, have been placed next to each other, and while the figures gaze up and down at each other, creating an appealing illusion of interactivity, in fact they can't see each other, let alone be recognized. This, the much-heralded "multi-dynamic image technique," had been debuted in the Canadian director Christopher Chapman's 1967 film *A Place to Stand*, which collages a varying number up to fifteen panes of footage, condensing an hour and a half's worth of film into eighteen or so minutes. Steve McQueen, supposedly at the opening screening of Chapman's movie, appeared the following year in

1.7 At the end of the introduction to *The Brady Bunch*, Ann B. Davis, as Alice, appears in the center of the grid, smiling forward at the camera. The text reads, "and Ann B. Davis as Alice."

Norman Jewison's artsy heist movie *The Thomas Crown Affair*, which made extensive use of the Chapman technique; nonetheless, by some point in the 1970s, it was known as "the Brady Bunch effect." But what *is* the effect, exactly? To isolate the unitary components of a "bunch," presenting no model of convergence but an image of absolute isolation within the family, overlaid with the simulacrum of interaction, with no eye contact? Or perhaps, in its very anachronism, to depict the family as an accretion of incompatible temporalizations, a palimpsest of unlike individuals?

For some time, one watches the eight individuals bob their heads and explore the lines of nonconnection that the viewer's eye can nonetheless be fooled into thinking look like a real family, around a black square—a patch of screen in quantum oscillation between figure and ground, the black square either a semantic void around which the family is to be gathered or the darkness and isolation from which family provides an escape, an undecidable "either/or" rather than a more comfortable "both/and." Yet the void is eventually populated, by a figure whose presence in the Bunch is a matter of contingency, whose identity has not been disclosed in the song, and whose appearance bridges the visual distinction between blonde loveliness and manly loneliness.

1.8 In a still from *Sitcom*, Nicolas, Sophie, and their mother float in a swimming pool.

Surely Ann B. Davis, who never married and who was not recorded to have made any investments in heterosexuality, belongs in a different universe from the Bunch. It is as though, during a game of *Hollywood Squares*, a third contestant has appeared who insists on marking the center square with neither a naught nor a cross but with some arcane and incomprehensible sigil. Alice beams out her self-sufficiency to a relieved camera, while Marcia, Greg, Bobby, and eventually all of them look at her, and then perhaps at each other through her. Patricia White has observed that figures of butch competence are intrinsic to the logic by which compulsory heterosexuality persuades itself to soldier mordantly onward in classic Hollywood cinema, but this crucial position of a figure for whom even the term *lesbian* feels like a sort of euphemism, in one of postwar American culture's most ubiquitous diagrams of heterosexuality, has not lost its power to disarm those who watch the sequence for the first time.[8] Of course, for Alice herself (waged reproductive worker: servant), the heterosexual grid is a prison: no way out for her of a swarm that bunches around her like a closet.

A brief shot in *Sitcom*, shortly before the climactic sequence, figures post-familial relation as a free-floating movement, backgrounded by a grid of black lines against blue, that neither binds nor frames.

Tool *Gleichzeitigkeit*

Yet if the sitcom's renegotiation of public and private spheres of economic activity seems to transpire within the domain of woman, one could not conclude that the genre upholds any more general feminization of labor. Indeed, perhaps perversely, several sitcoms have treated the domestic sphere as, properly speaking, the space of patriarchal governance par excellence. Such stoical reterritorializations can transmit from an armchair, in which one might find an Archie Bunker; from a couch, on which the browbeaten Al Bundy (same initials) resists the sexual advances of his glamazon wife, Peggy, and the (trans-?) feminization threatened by her uncastrated desire; or from the shed, in which men's toys and tools, the instrumentation of masculine reproductive labor, can be exhibited in all their violent glory. From the shed, Tim Allen in *Home Improvement* deploys a militant offensive to smash asunder domesticity and femininity, in the name of a barbarian, redcap masculinity. Be it coincidence, prefiguration, or glitch in the matrix, an alarming proportion of the audience in Tim Allen's 1990s show-within-a-show seems to be sporting our own epoch's armband, and one of them looks unmistakably like Tucker Carlson.

The first episode of *Home Improvement* opens with a close-up on a television screen, on which is playing footage of a soundstage made up to look like a toolshed and into which walks Tim Allen, playing a character named "Tim." Then, the camera retracts from the screen to display Tim Allen watching himself on television, on a soundstage made up to look like an open-plan living room and kitchen. If the mirror stage depends on the simultaneity of the conscious experience of sensation and its objective depiction, *Home Improvement* opens onto a television stage in which there is only lag. Larry Sanders is always watching himself on TV, as are BoJack Horseman and, in a more ambivalent way, Sarah Lynn. Here is Tim as "Tim" watching "Tim," but any ruptures that might have been

1.9 Peggy and Al Bundy (Katey Sagal and Ed O'Neill) pose in a press image from *Married . . . with Children.*

1.10 Audience members of *Tool Time*, Tim Allen's show-within-a-show in *Home Improvement*, laugh at the camera. Several are wearing red baseball caps.

opened up by these folds of perspective and identity are mobilized at once in an impatient opening shot that pans, with Tim, leftward, as he opens a door at the back of the set to beckon his kids in from the garden with "my show's on"; the camera then moves, in a quick POV double take, across to Tim's wife, Jill, who is struggling with an ironing board in a semi-illuminated alcove at the upstage-leftmost corner of the set.

"Couldn't get the boys to watch, huh?"

"They were a little busy."

"So am I." In a virtuosic gesture, she unfolds the ironing board and plants it like a flag on the kitchen linoleum.

The shot has worked to question, and then to resolve, the problem of simultaneity between subject and object—the establishment of what the anthropologist Johannes Fabian called *"Gleichzeitigkeit,"* which he translated into English with the cumbersome "coevalness" but that refers more properly to the phenomenological condition of assuming a shared temporality with someone else—in Fabian's case, the anthropological other, the *denial* of whose *Gleichzeitigkeit* constitutes the basis of anthropology as a modern science.[9] The question of a sexual *Gleichzeitigkeit,* and of sex as a possible vehicle for racial *Gleichzeitigkeit,* turns out to be key to the episode's major theme: the domestic sphere as a space of contest between men and women, a contest that will eventually take the form of a fight over Tim's desire to endow the dishwasher spray with "more power," thus vitiating the apparent need for him to rinse the trace of egg yolk off his plate before washing it. Predating Susan Faludi's book *Stiffed: The Betrayal of the American Man* (1999) by eight years, *Home Improvement* presented a man worn down by the comforts of postwar domesticity, seeking rejuvenation in DIY culture, which he figures as a masculine reclamation of reproductive work.

Boy, there's nothing like the feeling of rawhide and cold steel hanging on your hips. My wife says when I put this bad boy on, I turn into a wild, hairy, disgusting ape—[*he grunts*]—You know what? I don't think women understand the feeling of rawhide and steel vise-gripping monkey pliers, dado head cut, flat jig, miter jig, box hat, glue ... [*more grunting*].

The remasculinization of the American man would require his adornment in a new, beastlier uniform, whose itemizable parts each seem to speak suggestively of animality and phallic wholeness. Yet the masturbatory procedure, which was apparent long before the accelerating list climaxed in "glue" and grunting, coincides with a progressive sense of evolutionary reversal, man into ape, as though the fluid with which Tim is splashing himself is not just semen but originary protoplasm.

Tim's enigmatic neighbor Wilson (whose bottom half is curiously unavailable to the camera, first obscured by a wooden door he is fashioning and later by the garden fence over which Tim speaks to him, which covers everything south of the nose) offers him a historical theory of male rejuvenation: "You see, Tim, the Industrial Revolution took the adult male out of the home. Boys were left without an older man to teach them how to be men. We need to get back to something more primitive, atavistic." At this point, Tim reignites his grunt, leaning into its seductive quality. Wilson's name recalls an earlier sitcom neighbor, George Wilson of *Dennis the Menace*, which debuted in 1959, but his theory depends on the restitution of a much older way of things, from the morass of ethnographic time on the other side of *Gleichzeitigkeit*: "Men need to spend more time around the campfire with their elders, like in ancient days, seeking wisdom, telling stories, sharing." The shared whiteness of Tim and Wilson—and, indeed, of his wife, Jill; kids, Brad, Randy, and Mark; brothers, Marty and Jeff; coworker Al; and almost all the shown audience of *Tool Time*—locates this discourse within the context of white envy: an imitation of generalizable indigeneity, diluted to the point of absolute vacuity.

That Wilson's fake-native design for life cannot be taken seriously is never really in doubt: Jill has no luck getting the job she had applied for (they called and left a message with her husband), and Tim's souped-up dishwasher blasts a hole through the back of the kitchen island—an image foreboding, perhaps, the frantic relation to anal eroticism that the episode establishes. The case for remasculinizing reproductive labor collapses in the light of patriarchy, which arranges everything for Tim's convenience and even allows him a richly compensated simulacrum of unwaged housework in the form of his show, *Tool Time*—a little like Marie Antoinette's farm at Versailles. Yet the sublimation of that fantasy seems to emerge in the pilot episode's many explorations of anal eroticism, which allow Tim access to the masochistic *and* the sadistic elements of his desire to find a masculine role as a domestic caregiver. The masochistic side, plainly enough, can be offered only to a wife who cannot threaten him—she slaps his ass and he responds, "Do the other side! Oh, I'm your love slave!"—but the sadistic side can be deployed more gleefully, and with all the tools at his disposal, against the men whose intimacy has been eroded by the passage of time: "I think we oughta start today by spackling Al's butt crack shut, huh? With the new Patch-N-Paint butt crack filler putty. Hey, I smell voltage. I think it's time to drill." The unspoken solution to Tim's problem would entail his wife being, or becoming, an object of the same "primitive" lust that, at present, compels him toward the cracks of his male acquaintances (butt and fence) and that requires "more power" to drill through. But obviously no woman worth drilling would allow herself, even imaginatively, to be spackled in the butt crack like Al, Tim's beta cuck assistant. Hence the offstaging of pleasure into the shed—and even more covertly, into the *set* of a shed—where men can understand each other. He tells Jill he'll only be at Sears for twenty minutes.

"Twenty minutes, who are you kidding?" she replies. "You'll be down there drooling, fondling all the tools, your eyes buggin' out. You don't even look at me like that."

"I would if you were two speeds and reversible," Tim responds.

Loving

Richard and Mildred Loving left Virginia for Washington, DC, in June 1958, got married there, and returned to their home in Virginia, where they were charged by a grand jury, pleaded guilty, and were sentenced to a year in prison each, to be suspended for twenty-five years on the condition that they leave Virginia and not return together for the duration.[10] Having gotten married out of state was no defense against Virginia's statutory scheme against interracial marriage, not just because it indicated an intention to evade Virginian law but because, according to §20–58 of the Virginia code:

> *If* any white person and colored person shall go out of this State, for the purpose of being married, and with the intention of returning, and be married out of it, and afterwards return to and reside in it, cohabiting as man and wife, they shall be punished as provided in § 20–59, and the marriage shall be governed by the same law as if it had been solemnized in this State. The fact of their cohabitation here as man and wife shall be evidence of their marriage.[11]

The law thus depends on the creation of a category distinct from legally recognizable marriage: "cohabitation [. . .] as man and wife." This category resembles occasional juridical concessions made to so-called common-law arrangements but with a key distinction: the cohabitation conjured by the Virginia statute exists to provide evidence of a marriage that the state *does not* recognize; indeed, one that the state criminalizes. Moreover, the law seems to endow the state with the power to declare certain marriages illegal—the statute does not stipulate that the Lovings' marriage would have been treated as though it were *established* in Virginia but as though it had been "solemnized" there. It would have been possible to assert that the marriage would have depended on what J. L. Austin would have called an "infelicitous" speech act, but instead the law seems to assume that the Lovings' criminality derived not from the falsity of their marriage but from its intrinsic properties. The "as man and wife" clause prefigures the notorious Section 28 of the UK Local Government Act 1988, which banned anyone from "promot[ing] the teaching in any maintained school of the acceptability of homosexuality as a pretended family relationship."[12] What the two clauses share is a desire not merely to prevent any legal recognition of sexual relationships the state finds odious but to criminalize the *representation* of those relationships in any way that could be construed to undermine the figurative necessity of social reproduction.

Historians tend to date the American television sitcom from the first episode of *Mary Kay and Johnny* in 1947, but a case could be made for *Amos 'n' Andy*, which didn't appear on television until 1951 but had been delivering almost identical scripts over the radio since 1928. Yet the migration from audio to visual format exposed the cathodic contradictions upon which the genre was being founded. Written by Charles Correll and Freeman Gosden, two white men who played the titular Black roles, *Amos 'n' Andy* was audio minstrelsy, a follow-up to another radio minstrelsy show by the same authors, *Sam 'n' Henry*, which was broadcast on Chicago radio between 1926 and 1927—the show's theme tune, "The Perfect Song," had been adapted from the score of *The Birth of a Nation*. The widespread popularity of these shows among white audiences was matched by a broad condemnation in the Black press of the racist stereotypes upon which they depended: the *Pittsburgh Courier* published a petition and several editorials denouncing the radio broadcast in 1931.[13] Yet as early as 1946, Correll and Gosden had tried to migrate the show onto television, running into a difficulty: their performances in the title roles had been partly responsible for the show's appeal, but for them to keep playing the roles on television, they would have had to adopt actual blackface rather than its audio imitation, which would have undermined the show's claims to working-class realism.[14] Eventually, the two performers delivered a theatrically self-pitying interview to the Associated Press in 1951, in which they admitted with a flourish that recasting Amos and Andy is professional suicide, but "by [1953] the wounded rhinoceros (radio) will probably have fallen dead anyway [. . .] and we're ready. We've both bought wheelchairs."[15] But lest any reader suspect that their decision to step down derived from any ambivalence about the anti-Black foundations of minstrelsy, Correll was quick to stipulate that the reason for their stepping down was only that "we don't look believable in blackface."[16] And of course, Correll and Gosden remained the writers of the TV adaptation, and the protests against their crude stereotypes only escalated, until advertisers walked; *Amos 'n' Andy* was canceled in 1953 and removed from syndication in 1966.

After cancelation in 1953, Correll and Gosden had an idea for a relaunch that might, they hoped, satisfy the various constituencies that CBS was trying to draw together. According to a report in *Jet* magazine, the relaunch "will show Gosden and Correll in one corner of the TV screen while Negro actors fill in the action."[17] This remarkable, and ultimately abortive, plan imagined the space of the television screen subject to the visual logic of segregation, a racial materialization of what W. E. B. Du Bois called "the color line."[18] Bringing together blackface minstrelsy and silent movie performance, and eerily echoing the sign-language interpreters who started appearing in a corner of television screens around 1950, the planned *Amos 'n' Andy* relaunch exposes the degree to which the spatial figuration of the television, the grid, arranged social contradictions, making visible to audiences conflicts that might otherwise have remained invisibly notional. The scarcity of interracial families in sitcoms, a genre predicated on heterosexuality as a blending process, is therefore less surprising than it might seem. One of the few such shows, *True Colors*, which ran from 1990 until 1992, was canceled partway through its second season, one of the central characters having been recast and the other actor having to skip recording after being diagnosed with fatal lung cancer. The white showrunner, Michael J. Weithorn, created *True Colors* after leaving the writing staff of *Family Ties*, a show in which Michael J. Fox played a young conservative at odds with his liberal parents—a much more manageable kind of blending, requiring neither white capacity for self-reflection nor buy-in from Black audiences, both of which were apparently missing from *True Colors*.

The exhilaration with which sitcoms celebrate motley nonetheless works to inhibit racial blending. One might think, too, of the alarming intensity of the patriarch's racist outrages in Wes Anderson's 2001 movie *The Royal Tenenbaums*. Not a sitcom, the movie nonetheless shares a number of conceptual and visual premises with the genre: a diverse family blended, seemingly, from different genre traditions; an adoption plot raising the question of incest; and perhaps above all, a formal interest in the aesthetic and political possibilities of the two-dimensional plane—in other words, a version of *The Addams Family*, with "spooky" switched out for "quirky," both of which belong in the *New Yorker*, in any case. The plot concerns an estranged father's attempts to prevent his ex-wife from marrying her Black accountant and friend, and while the movie displays more interest in the relationships Royal Tenenbaum (Gene Hackman) tries to rekindle with his sons, daughter, and grandsons, the romantic conflict between Royal and Henry Sherman (Danny Glover) is figured in primarily racial terms, from

1.11 The Tenenbaum family sits around a dining table in *The Royal Tenenbaums*.

the moment that Royal's old manservant Pagoda informs him of the news ("the black man asks her to be his wife") to the threatening, physically animated argument in which Royal repeatedly asks if Henry wants "to talk some jive."

The governing racial logic of familial blending might also explain why an otherwise conservative show can be so bold as to describe a family comprising a white gay couple with a baby adopted from Vietnam, a white straight couple, and a biracial straight couple as "modern." *I Love Lucy* and *The Addams Family*, of course, had both organized their domestic spaces around white women with Latino husbands yet had not been overcome by the fantasy of a weakened heterosexual matrix that they needed to develop a prophylactic rationale to maintain its grip on relationality as such. But just such a prophylactic device (albeit a spectacularly broken one) makes itself known from the start of *Modern Family*: the *modern* family is one that sustains a system for normalizing and containing homophobia, racism, and misogyny after the election of a Black president and the decriminalization of sodomy. The script for the show's pilot, in which it was to be called "My American Family," is signed "December 9th, 2008," just over a month after the election of Barack Obama, and might endure as the singular document of the "post-racial" ideology of neoliberalism as it was felt around that particular election. Early in the episode, the gay couple, Cameron and Mitchell (their names perhaps a reference to John Cameron Mitchell, the writer and star of *Hedwig and the Angry Inch*?), are

1.12 The cast of *Modern Family* wears all white and smiles from a giant gold frame.

dealing with fondly protective glances from the apparently heterosexual passengers on the plane from which they are bringing their newly adopted baby home from Vietnam. When the passengers realize that they are gay, an old woman looks horrified, a middle-aged man averts his eyes, and a blonde woman mutters to her husband, "Oh look at that baby with those cream puffs." Mitchell rears up defensively and delivers a racially grounded defense of their relationship: "This baby would have grown up in a crowded orphanage if it wasn't for us cream puffs. And you know what? Here's a note to all of you who judge: hear this. Love knows no race, creed, or gender— and shame on you, you small-minded, ignorant few—" before Cameron cuts him off to reveal that, in fact, the baby, whose new name ("Lily") signifies paradigmatic whiteness, is indeed grasping a creamy bun. It's a perfect moment for neoliberal post-racism: a generalized platitude about the interchangeability of identities is shown to have reflected nothing more than the prejudice of a fussy queer, and everyone can quickly forget the horror that rippled through the cabin only a few seconds prior. What kind of irony, then, that Mitchell's father, now married to a younger Colombian woman, made his fortune selling closets?

The Beaver's Father's Meerschaum

The boy next door is a postwar phenomenon, a product of the suburbanization of American cities. He (or she, the girl next door) promises to minimize the threat of exogamy: at the least, he will minimize the difference between us and the world that sex promises only to inflate; in the best-case scenario, we can merge our farms together, let fall the exogamic boundary, simply absorb property, with love, into the plot of our body. Their generalized similarity makes their differences stand out. Girls next door are developmentally advanced and therefore subject to pornographic spectatorship (binoculars in the treehouse, pardonable on the grounds of youthful curiosity). Her name locates her in the romance of colonial American landscape: Topanga, Willow, Donna Pinciotti. The boy next door is younger, nerdier, his unwelcome sexual advances pardonable on the grounds of dorkiness; even his name is cringey: Urkel, Roger, Skippy. Yet if the erotic purpose of the (object) next door is to act as training wheels on the bicycle of exogamy, the question of how to dispense with one's neighbor ethically lacks an obvious answer. Excluded from certain domestic practices but included in others, the child-neighbor haunts can penetrate even the most insulated familial ecosystem, an emissary, or even a spy, from another state—even the most insulated, by which I mean *Leave It to Beaver*, a sitcom that ran from 1957 to 1963. Despite the show's repute as moralistic nuclear propaganda, the Beaver's story twists with its own complexities, even before the sequels *Still the Beaver* and *The New Leave It to Beaver* depicted an adult Theodore "The Beaver" Cleaver (still played by Jerry Mathers) as a divorcé, having been divorced by a woman named Kimberly after she decided to pursue a career in veterinary medicine, and being left to raise their two children with his own mother. The origins of the Beaver's nickname remained obscure until the original show's finale in 1963, when his brother, Wally, admits to having derived it as a young child unable to pronounce "Theodore," lisping the name into "Tweeter," which then mutated into "Beaver." Mathers had claimed that the show's co-writer and co-creator, Joe Connelly, had known a Beaver in the Merchant Marines and that the writers retconned the "Tweeter" line after having had no idea why this child would be nicknamed so.[19] "Tweeter," like "Beaver," is listed in *Urban Dictionary* (though not in the *Oxford English Dictionary*) as a term for vagina; it's not impossible that the real-life Beaver earned his nickname with a beard, the term already in use for both vagina and facial hair since the turn of the century.[20] His name prophesies his future as a Mummy's boy, then: destined to leave his wife for his mother, to fumble the exogamic imperative, the Beaver never quite left the womb, nor even the house, whence he returns after the collapse of his marriage. By then, his father, Ward, has died offscreen: an Oedipal victory for the Beav, albeit one that costs him any hope of actual Oedipalization.

What, if anything, could be "left to" such a boy? The show's title, whether or not it is supposed to provoke a dirty laugh, opens a question of leaving and fails or refuses to close it. It could be a slightly sarcastic in-joke ("leave it to Beaver to mess this one up"), a testamentary declaration regarding the Cleavers' properties, or a more heartfelt statement of trust. Whichever, leaving the Beaver at home is one of Ward and June's most trusted parenting techniques, and, like the subject of the Irenaean theodicy, the child always learns the right lesson when he messes up. In the second-season episode "The Pipe," the Beaver is left with his neighbor Larry, and the two of them are left with the Beaver's father's meerschaum pipe, a gift sent in the mail from the Rutherfords, who are on holiday in Frankfurt. Ward doesn't smoke a pipe, so he won't have a chance to enjoy what the accompanying note refers to as the pipe's "rubescent chromaticity," but the changing color is among the many aspects of the pipe that might appeal to a younger crowd, and the pipe catches the eye of Beaver's friend Larry, who comes over and sweet-talks the boy into watching him smoke coffee grounds. The meerschaum is a fascinating object: bright white and ornate, it is both aperture and phallus, both something to be plugged and something to be inserted; like Larry's confident masculinity, the pipe is both compulsively fascinating to the Beaver and a source of nebulous shame. Beaver washes the coffee grounds out of the pipe after Larry leaves, but the smell of coffee—the smell of an older man—lingers long enough for Wally to notice. When Larry returns to the house, he has the mien of an addict: any hope that the coffee grounds might have left the pipe without stimulating any symptoms disappears.

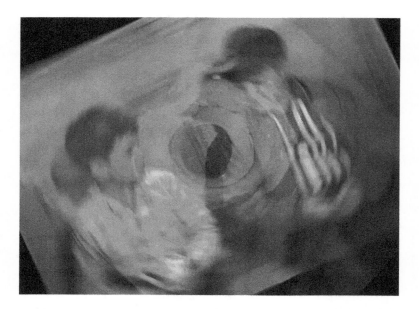

1.13 In a still from *Leave It to Beaver*, Beaver and Larry get dizzy after smoking a pipe.

His tone becomes hectoring as he insists that the Beaver smoke actual tobacco with him: the *neighbor*'s desire then transforms from an erotic problem to an ethical one. The Beav does indeed take a puff, while a hesitant laugh track communicates more panic than merriment, and the camera swirls around in a spin-wipe: a modest but unmistakable hallucination sequence, depicting a character's disoriented state of mind with an editing technique.

It is a faux pas. As a mere neighbor, and not a Cleaver, Larry has no obligation to assist Beaver with the cleanup, and his abandonment of the situation is as brutal as was his demand for companionship: "you better clean it up before they find out you been smoking." The problem is not just that Beaver has engaged in behavior that should have waited until he was twenty-one; the bigger issue is that by acceding to his neighbor's wishes, he seems to have entered into a compact of secrecy incompatible with his membership in the family. The Beaver's crime was therefore against the family rather than against his own body; suspicion for having "gesmoken" the meerschaum naturally falls on the elder brother, Wally, putting Beaver in the position of having to choose between shopping his friend, who has taken advantage of the law of hospitality without being bound by it, and preserving his blameless brother's reputation. It's no choice at all, especially after Mr. Cleaver regales his sons with the story of Pandora's box—a bowl without a mouthpiece. The father has attempted to heterosexualize the transgression when he projects this story onto Wally, but the pipe itself tells a different story: as the Beaver learns from his mother, far from "rubescent," the pipe "turns brown when you smoke it," which compels the younger brother to confess all, at last overcome with guilt over Wally's being scapegoated. Yet the law of hospitality requires one final betrayal of the Beaver: when his father asks him if Larry put him up to smoking the pipe, the Beaver lies to protect his friend: "No, sir, we put each other up to it." His father appreciates the Beaver's gallantry, but to the viewer this can only be a lie. On the upside, at least Beaver has learned enough from the experience that by the end of the episode he can remark that "if grown-ups say it was so bad, there must be something real good about it," even if it is solely to recant the idea. The moral delivered from husband to wife after the kids have retired suggests a greater knowledge of the situation than he had seemed to possess: "one of the unwritten rules of childhood: no use in doing anything bad unless there's someone there to admire you for it."

Drug plots like this early example in *Leave It to Beaver* allow writers to explore the ethical obligations specific to childhood and to rehearse in didactic terms the general case for family-based models of belonging. Larry, ultimately, wasn't one of us, and the episode's conclusion is that the Cleaver brothers should look out for each other. A related plot recurs in an influential early episode of *The Cosby Show* titled "Theo and the Joint," which was broadcast in 1985 and is part of the class of "very special episodes" that peaked in the 1980s, in which sitcoms would dedicate a particular episode to didactic instruction around a social issue—drugs being the most common, but *Boy Meets World* covered pedophilia and cult brainwashing; *Diff'rent Strokes* covered pedophilia; *Full House* covered anorexia, and so on. *South Park*, meanwhile, satirizes the conspicuous moralizing of these episodes whenever Kyle says, "You know, I learned something today," before spouting some argumentative pablum. "Theo and the

Joint," however, was an oddity: Theo Huxtable's (Malcolm-Jamal Warner) parents find a marijuana cigarette in one of his schoolbooks; Theo denies that it is his, saying he doesn't know where it came from. Cliff (Bill Cosby) and Clair (Phylicia Rashad) take him at his word, but Theo remains anxious that he is arousing suspicion, so he confronts the guy at school who stashed the weed, a muscular boy named Tony Braxton, and threatens to fight him if he doesn't come home with him and communicate that he was the guilty party. After he has done so, Cliff repeats that he had believed his son but also communicates pride at Theo having stood up to a tough-looking kid, and Cliff tells Tony Braxton, "I think you have a problem," urging him to talk to his parents or a counselor. In this case, the law of hospitality works slightly differently: Theo's courage, which derived from the strong family bonds his parents have fostered, has allowed him to be useful to someone *outside* the family unit. Theo has become a kind of Cosby missionary; the Beaver remains, for better and worse, solidly a Cleaver until the end.

Whither Urkel?

The appearance of Steve Urkel in the twelfth episode of *Family Matters*, one of the longest-running and most syndicated sitcoms to focus on an African American family, dramatically reoriented the show's premise and its setting. Initially a spin-off from *Perfect Strangers* focused on a blue-collar cop named Carl Winslow and his family, *Family Matters* in effect became a spin-off from itself after audiences responded warmly to Urkel, a nerdy boy from a neighboring family who was initially introduced as a romantic mismatch for the eldest daughter, Laura Winslow, and who eventually became the show's main focus. In one sense, Urkel's success illustrates a general principle of sitcom narrative: that it is difficult to derive a serial comedy plot from a family without introducing some external element—indeed, of the period's other successful Black-centered sitcoms, *The Cosby Show* was unusual for focusing solely on one family—though as we have seen, it's a family with a mission: *The Fresh Prince of Bel-Air* depicted the out-of-water experiences of a Philadelphia teen-

1.14 In an episode of *Family Matters*, Laura Winslow looks down at an unrolled paper towel roll dragged across the floor by Steve Urkel, who wears suspenders.

ager sent to live with his tony California relatives, and *Sister, Sister* is the story of two twins separated at birth, who find each other as teenagers and attempt to build a family together with one's mother and the other's father. Yet Urkel's position in *Family Matters* was, in another sense, quite unique: here was the central character of a family sitcom who bore no family ties to anyone else, whose presence in each episode is felt primarily as an unwelcome imposition. Among Urkel's many characteristic tics, one is asking whether the Winslows have "got any cheese?"; another is asking, "Did I do that?" after accidentally breaking one of their home furnishings. Yet if Urkel is unwelcome at the Winslows' house, he is no more welcome in his own—we learn, eventually, that his parents dislike him so much that they have moved to Russia—and when combined with his extravagant personal manner, which is undersold by the word *nerd*, his uncertain provenance marks him out as a kind of changeling boy, a surrogate fairy boy, who occupies the family setting as part-defective son and part-defective romantic prospect.

From the start, Urkel's queerness introduces disorder into the otherwise law-loving scene of a police officer, his odd-jobbing wife, and their three kids. Or perhaps, rather, he simply reflects back the family's intrinsic disorder. To that extent, Urkel is positioned as the "identified patient" of the Winslow family, to use a term developed by the anthropologist Gregory Bateson. The identified patient, tasked with the role of maintaining what Bateson called "family homeostasis," symptomatizes as embodied difference the relational contradictions and pathologies of a family "when the family lack the resources for morphogenesis," that is, for creating, adapting, and sustaining forms of relation adequate to the sustenance of social order.[21] The anti-psychiatric practitioner R. D. Laing took the notion one step further. Rather than simply externalizing the pathologies of a dysfunctional family, Laing and his coauthor Aaron Esterson held that "schizophrenia" was *invariably* a response to pathological features of the so-called normal family itself.[22] Just as in the Book of Leviticus Aaron designates one of a pair of goats a scapegoat and imbues it with the sins and transgressions of Israel, so the family, without consciously deciding upon whom, designates one member as the identified patient, who is thereafter treated as the sick one, while (according to Laing) the pathology dwells in the family as such rather than its members, and least of all in the one being singled out.

"Laura's First Date," the episode in which Urkel first appears, presents a plot delicately balanced on the cusp of sexual and familial affiliations: the family's daughter, Laura, has turned thirteen and wants to go on her first date to a dance. In order to show support and control the outcome, respectively, Laura's brother, Eddie, and father both supply her with suitors: a cool kid named Tyrone; and the "mouse eater" Steve Urkel, to whom everyone immediately refers by his last name. Unknown to either, however, Laura has summoned up the courage to ask her actual crush, a boy named Mark, to the dance, and he has accepted the offer, thwarting the plots of brother, father, Urkel, and Tyrone. Mark is a stranger figure than the characters seem to acknowledge: despite being, one assumes, no older than fourteen, he comports himself in a manner almost cartoonishly *normal*, as if to mirror Urkel's chaotic and theatrical presentation of self. "Hi, I'm Mark Newhouse," he says, making his first entrance onto the set, his name, blazer, and manner all strangely reminiscent of a thirtysomething newlywed. Mark's bizarro normalness is not the episode's only moment of successfully domesticated queer panic: it had opened on Eddie standing on the kitchen counter in one of Laura's pink dresses, their aunt correcting the stitching and fit around him while he pouted. But more striking is the family's conspicuous disgust at Urkel: the episode ends with the Winslows shuddering while thinking about him, as disincentive to Carl to attempt any further matchmaking for his daughter. The abortive romantic plot between Laura and the mouse eater (an image that, in the context of a narrative of sexual maturation, might cause one to think of a tampon) functioned as a cipher, then, merely to convey Urkel from his initial role as exterior misfit in relation to Laura to his true place as an abject proxy for Carl. And it is indeed this role that Urkel increasingly comes to play in the lives of the Winslows: not merely unwelcome suitor but unwanted fairy son.

One of the most well-known episodes of *Family Matters*—it was the subject of a parodic *Saturday Night Live* short released online in 2015—is the fifth season's "Dr. Urkel and Mr. Cool," the title a reference to Robert Louis Stevenson's gothic novella concerning a physician who transforms himself into a monster by drinking an experimental potion. Like Stevenson's novel, the episode explores the meanings of physical transformation and the strange collusion of mental and social phenomena that such transformations effectuate. At the episode's opening, Urkel's clumsiness upsets Laura—whose sexual favor he has been seeking now in each of ninety-odd episodes—and she asks him, "Why are you the way you are?" His answer is, essentially, "genes"; he mentions "chromosomes" early on in the episode and describes the physical condition of the symptomatic body as one indelibly encoded in the basic material components of his body. Though perhaps unfixable, these "genes" were not originally resistant to physical deformation: following Urkel's "genes" explanation, Laura asks, "But what happened to yours?" and Urkel replies, "Well, it may have something to do with the fact that the day before I was conceived, a road flare went off in my father's pocket." A jarringly risqué joke for a family show, the "road flare" explanation proposes that Urkel's awkwardness derived from the primary emasculation of his father, or at least that Urkel believes that it might have. Among the gendering effects of that claim—a narrative of the kind that Freud might group under the heading of "childhood sexual theories"—one derives the sense not merely that Urkel understands the way he is as fundamentally a *sexual* malformation but, moreover, that the malformation is not even, truly, his. Like the symptoms of an identified patient, Urkel's manner expresses not his own injury but someone else's. Family matters indeed.

In order to assuage Laura's frustration at the way he is, Urkel develops a potion, isolating the "cool gene" whose latent presence in his system is obscured by the gene for "nasal drip." Synthesizing and multiplying this gene, Urkel develops a potion that, when drunk, will transform him into someone "cool"—though the sexual difficulties of this coercive therapy become apparent before he even drinks it. Urkel boasts, "I might even sprout a chest hair or two," and Laura replies drily, "First, you better sprout a chest." To the extent that the potion will enact a masculinizing puberty on Urkel's body, it will have to bypass or sublimate the prior unsexedness of his latent form—and indeed, the injunction to "sprout a chest" redirects the phallic energies of the chest hair into a description of something that sounds suspiciously like a *feminizing* puberty.

One might observe, too, that the awkwardness that Urkel seeks to dispel is shaped in part by the series' variable positioning of the character in relation to the social field of Blackness. In "Laura's First Date," the three suitors were arranged into a sexual hierarchy that interacted in complex ways with the episode's depiction of familial intimacy: Tyrone, Eddie's choice of date, is clearly positioned as the sexiest prospect but also, by virtue of his proximity to Eddie, perversely the least suitable—a proxy for a family member, Tyrone gives a performance of young Black masculinity that marks him as kin. Although Urkel's self-presentation could not be easily aligned with white performances of self—unlike, say, Will's frequent barbs at Carlton in *Fresh Prince*—it is clearly exogamic, and the wince that the Winslows share at the end of the episode partly derives from a shared horror at letting one of *them* near the family ever again. Mark Newhouse, the proxy bourgeois homemaker, arrives as the perfectly medio-gamic beau, if the coinage makes sense:

1.15 Bill Cosby wears one of his signature sweaters as Cliff Huxtable in *The Cosby Show*.

he seems to be from another family *like* the Winslows but distinct from them. In fact, in his comically well-comported suit and tie, he almost looks like an emissary from *The Cosby Show*, whose protagonist, Cliff Huxtable, was well known for his own conspicuously cozy style of dress, and whose lead actor, Bill Cosby, in 2004 delivered the famous "Pound Cake" speech, excoriating Black Americans for the moral implications of their style of dress and post-*Roots* naming conventions:

> Are you not paying attention, people with their hat on backwards, pants down around the crack. Isn't that a sign of something, or are you waiting for Jesus to pull his pants up? Isn't it a sign of something when she's got her dress all the way up to the crack . . . and got all kinds of needles and things going through her body. What part of Africa did this come from? We are not Africans. Those people are not Africans, they don't know a damned thing about Africa. With names like Shaniqua, Shaligua, Mohammed and all that crap and all of them are in jail.[23]

1.16 Jaleel White as Urkel's cool alter ego, Stefan Urquelle, in *Family Matters*.

The transformation of awkward Steve Urkel into über-cool Stefan Urquelle, however, triggers in the character a newly confident performance of precisely the kind of Black masculinity Cosby despises. Stefan is magnetic, apparently literally: when he walks into a party in his loose-fitting white suit, the throng of kids seems physically drawn to his body as it moves around the room, and the flock of fans that he's assembled comprises representatives of a wide range of sexual, racial, and gendered social codes. Stefan emerges into the party less as Theo Huxtable and more as early-1990s Michael Jackson, healing the world around desire for his own transformed body.

The plot resolves with Laura becoming dissatisfied with Stefan and wishing Steve back, because of Stefan's self-serving egomania; Stefan has retained a pill containing anti-cool genes, and eventually he transforms back, although Stefan will make several future appearances on the show, in such moments when his sexual and psychosocial charisma can be useful to Urkel. The homeostatic force of sitcom narrative remains irresistible, and however improbable one finds Laura's stated preference for Steve over Stefan, it is a generic necessity. Yet to say the obvious, trans people will find much to recognize in the story of a young man who takes synthetic "genes" in order to intensify (or thwart) the effects of puberty—Steve Urkel, testo junkie—only to find that his own attempts to transform and heal, however sexually magnetic, fail to win the hearts of those whose neuroses he has been positioned to symptomatize. We might characterize Stefan Urquelle's condition as a presentation of the transmasculine double bind: compelled by ineligibility for the sexual market to pursue the physical transformation of masculinizing puberty, Urquelle discovers that indeed, transition works. Yet he also realizes that his own social position depends on the very discomfort for which he had been scapegoated and that by refusing to continue to perform that role, and seeking instead his own happiness, he has distanced himself from the social structures into which he was seeking entry. In that sense, we might observe that just as Urkel emerges as the identified patient of the Winslows, so the trans subject emerges as the identified patient of the sitcom: scapegoated into symptomatizing the contradictoriness of a system that has elected to despise it, the trans subject's fate depends on not merely a change of sex but a change of genre.

Nanu Nanu!

"Women are trouble—I should know, I've been one for two weeks!" Kristen Johnston's performance as Sally Solomon unashamedly embodies a range of stereotypes of trans women: she is prone to violence, sexually dominating, and auto-eroticizing but also prone to explosions of emotional overwhelm. The conceit of *Third Rock from the Sun* assumes a primary transsexuality as an effect of mind-body dualism. Before their arrival on Earth, the Solomon family were members of a hermaphroditic, and seemingly ageless, alien species; when they manifest in human bodies, then, their attentions are drawn to the sexual specificities of the organisms they are inhabiting: Sally notices her womanhood, while Tommy Solomon (a young Joseph Gordon-Levitt) notices that he appears to be a teenage boy, going through puberty, and perpetually fascinated by the feminized bodies he ogles in every scene. The Solomons' experiences of embodiment, then, are compensatory by definition: any such experience is noticeable only to the extent that it deviates from the originary unparticularized plenitude that governs the characters' experiences of consciousness. Transsexual by necessity, Sally is both a woman-in-a-man's-body and a man-in-a-woman's-body, the archon of a global transsexual regime that conditions not merely her intuitive experiences but the relationships that develop between her and the world. Her love interest, Officer Don (Wayne Knight), always looks up at her—Johnston is six feet tall, the same height as Allison Janney, her costar in later seasons of the sitcom *Mom*—and their chemistry nudges the show out of its generic habitation and into a screwball-inflected noir pastiche: the only moments when the otherwise consistently broad comedy sharpens into something with higher stakes. Yet notwithstanding the remarkable success of Johnston's performance as Sally, the remarkable aspect of *Third Rock from the Sun* is the degree to which its cosmological conceits affirm principles intrinsic to sitcom familiarization since the genre's inception. Sally and Tommy are attempting to make sense of bodies whose hormonal and plastic morphologies strike them as disorienting and original, but so too were Lucille Ball and Dick Van Dyke. It would therefore be misleading to describe *Third Rock*'s model of compensatory sexuation as deriving from gender stereotypes: the Solomons' experience affirms that embodiment is something that happens to us, a process not just of meaning-making but of materialization, which we are unable to resist even as we can negotiate its transcription into personality, relationality, and so on.

Alien sitcoms originated alongside the spooky and supernatural sitcoms, and *Third Rock* has an obvious forerunner: *My Favorite Martian*, which debuted in 1963, a year before *Bewitched* and *The Addams Family*. The show depicted a friendly relationship between a young journalist and his "Uncle Martin," in reality a Martian observer. Like Dick Solomon (John Lithgow), Ray Walston's Martian was not merely an observer, though, but a figure of intellectual incomprehension, whose tendency to analyze situations abstractly led him to underestimate the powers of luck, sentimentality, and so on. His primary relationship is with his young roommate Tim (Bill Bixby), whom he serves as a kind of virtuosic butler, eternally

1.17 A still from the introduction to *My Favorite Martians*. Two figures in collared shirts and sweaters appear in an oval window against a light-blue background.

generating new inventions to help with a new writing assignment—often, in *Bill and Ted* style, by time traveling to the relevant point in American history. Also like Dick Solomon, the Marti[a]n was a professor—in his case, of anthropology specializing in human history. But while the earlier character seems to have internalized scholarly methodologies, Dick's academic training seems to have been reduced to an alarmingly accurate pastiche of awkward middle-aged male professors' senses of humor, which Lithgow mercilessly reproduces. The female leads of both *Third Rock* and *My Favorite Martian* also primarily date police officers, who are positioned as hostile snoops into family affairs. The matching interventions of the criminal justice apparatus seem more than a mere coincidence: cops, as representatives of the state, threaten to expose the family disguise. Yet in so far as the family in *My Favorite Martian* takes the form of an intimate relationship between two men, pretending to be uncle and nephew, the cop necessarily appears bearing the authority of the antihomosexual Californian penal code: sodomy, or "sex perversion," as it was named in the code, was illegal until the relevant statutes were repealed in 1975.[24]

My Favorite Martian, however, was considered safe enough that it was adapted into a children's cartoon, *My Favorite Martians*, a few years after its cancelation in 1966, which was coincidentally three months before the riot at Compton's Cafeteria, San Francisco, which has been credited with establishing antihomophobic and antitransphobic activism in California.[25] The cartoon adaptation deploys the bright, polychromatic palette familiar to viewers of *Scooby-Doo*, which debuted in 1969, and introduced a second Martian, who offered some line of defense between young Tim and his magical "uncle" but made visible instead the spectacle of two "uncles," living together without any interest in heterosexual social formation. The cartoon's theme tune left open the nature of the Martians' relationship as well as their particular forms of embodied difference, the better to articulate a generalizable statement of liberal affirmation, which nonetheless chafes against the joyful queerness of the imagery itself:

> Now they've got special power
> and it makes some people wonder
> but only Tim and Katie
> really really know for sure
> that they're my favorite Martians
> you won't believe the things they do
> they're my favorite Martians
> and you're gonna love them too."

The Martians themselves seem to be wearing outfits from *The Boys in the Band* (1970).

Uncle Martin also formed the model for Mork from Ork (Robin Williams), who was initially a guest star on an episode of *Happy Days* in 1978 before getting his own show later that year. In *Happy Days*, Mork had manifested as a familiar type of threat: he wanted to kidnap Richie Cunningham and take him back to Ork, where he would no doubt have been subject to the "anal probe" given to Eric Cartman, among the many other gay-panicking hysterics down the decades. But in order to get his own show, Mork needed to be

1.18 Mork (Robin Williams) and Mindy (Pamela Dawber) sit on a paisley-printed couch in an episode of *Mork and Mindy*.

heterosexualized, and so he is sent from 1950s Milwaukee, Wisconsin, to "the future" of 1970s Boulder, Colorado. *Mork and Mindy* therefore commits itself to two contrary goals: to domesticate Mork within a heterosexual familial grid and to affirm his difference from those around him in liberal terms. Thus, Mindy's family is often too "conservative" to understand or appreciate Mork's oddball ways, as though he were simply a hippie or a Democrat rather than an alien. His more obvious human counterpart is a character named Exidor (Robert Donner), a visionary mystic who recognizes Mork as an alien and whose personal eccentricities (worshipping O. J. Simpson, addressing a gaggle of invisible converts) allow Mork, for once, to play the straight guy. The fantasy that an alien can save heterosexuality from its own contradictions, from ALF to *Lilo & Stitch*, imagines relatively little future for the alien himself: he remains like Bobby in another meta-sitcom, Stephen Sondheim's Broadway musical *Company*, the essential supplement.[26] What would we do without you?

PART 2
FRIENDS

She had broken off all relations with her friends with an abruptness that was foreign to her usual considerate nature.

"Isn't it depressing to live like this? I should become melancholy."

She laughed merrily in answer. No, quite the contrary. It was great to be alone again, free to come and go as one pleased. She was happy because her wings were not bound by distracting encounters, truly glad to be a single woman again. She had her work and needed nothing else. Life was so delightful, so exquisitely, captivatingly delightful!

ALEXANDRA KOLLONTAI, *A Great Love*

Hey Hey!

Over time, emotional bonds weaken. Over a long enough period, the story goes, they will have weakened to nothing. What might seem like an unfortunate problem for heterosexuality actually proves its necessity: in the absence of such bonds, we are left with institutional structures, and in the words of Laurie Anderson, "when love is gone, there's always justice / and when justice is gone, there's always force / and when force is gone, there's always Mom."[1] Anderson's words propose a rhetoric of diminishment that ends where everything started, each developmental phase a process of divestment, progress, and reversal of the same gesture. "O Superman," whatever other stories it is trying to tell us, communicates an idea about serial recursion, drawing in the Friedrich Nietzsche evoked by the song's title no less than the comic book character, though also chapter 38 of the *Tao Te Ching*:

> When Tao is lost, there is goodness.
> When goodness is lost, there is kindness.
> When kindness is lost, there is justice.
> When justice is lost, there is ritual.
> Now ritual is the husk of faith and loyalty,
>   the beginning of confusion.[2]

Yet in sitcoms, the gradual impoverishment and institutionalization of bonds (*not* of affect) is nothing to be feared; indeed, while the Beaver scurries home to Mom after the collapse of his exogamic experiment, the genre's retreat from the family home into the primordial swamps of young adulthood permits the formulation of a specific kind of tact whereby Mom withdraws from the scene at least temporarily. The possibility for setting a sitcom in that vacated space occurred to Bob Rafelson and Bert Schneider around 1965, and the following year *The Monkees* appeared, a sitcom without a situation, or at least a sitcom in which neither the family form nor the marriage plot has taken any root whatsoever.

Rafelson's model for the show was the Beatles movie *A Hard Day's Night*, which had been released in 1964, but that movie too was steeped in the script traditions of British sitcoms: along with the Fab Four, it costarred Wilfrid Brambell, who played the lead in *Steptoe and Son*, the British template for *Sanford and Son*; Norman Rossington, from *The Army Game* and the *Carry On* comedy movies; and John Junkin, who had guest-starred in Tony Hancock's eponymous ITV show. So not only was *The Monkees* a vehicle for introducing the exuberance of post-Beatles pop culture into American television; it was just as directly a method of globalizing the American sitcom, drawing on British and European formal tech-

2.1 Four young men—the Monkees—with long brown hair smile in a black-and-white publicity photo from *The Monkees*.

niques and practices. Not all the innovations were Anglicisms. *The Monkees* remains celebrated for its introduction of Stan Brakhage-inspired experimental editing techniques into prime-time television, yet where Brakhage's painted stock and variable exposure times worked to capture glimpses of fleeting urban environments, Rafelson trained his camera on the radiance of four handsome young men: sometimes rivals, sometimes intimates, sometimes interchangeable. At times, the show veers out of sitcom entirely into a kind of experimental softcore. The Monkees' 1968 film *Head*, which Rafelson cowrote with a young Jack Nicholson, forgoes sitcom altogether in favor of disconnected vignettes, some of which reference other movies (David Lean's *Lawrence of Arabia* and Stanley Kubrick's *Paths of Glory* among them) and some of which articulate a genially satirical relation to genre, such as when Micky Dolenz comes across an empty vending machine while walking thirstily through a desert.

The show's other innovation was its playful demolition of the spatial orthodoxies of the sitcom set. Filmed on a Columbia Pictures soundstage, a Hollywood address for the Monkees' "pad" was published in the teen magazine *16 Magazine*: 1334 North Beechwood Drive, Hollywood, CA, with minor, possibly accidental, variations on that address appearing in the show's scripts. Maps of the pad circulated widely too. Diegetically, the pad possessed delightful magical properties: a door to the side of the kitchen sometimes leads outside and sometimes to a closet; sometimes a hiding place and sometimes an escape route. The Monkees' pad is a domestic space freed from the rigorous architectural constructions of the family sitcom, and most episodes of the show contain a montage sequence in which the four lads simply scamper around the space, interacting with each other and with the environment in increasingly madcap ways. Indeed, the pad appeared altogether exempt from the rigorous temporalizations of heterosexual chronology: the Monkees were not so much premarriage as nonmarriage; the utopia they had sought was already present, in the details and the meanings that flashed between them in the California sun.

In the shadow of the family, there emerged an alternative practice of social constellation: the group of friends. Inhabiting the circuitous autotelic temporality of the sitcom rather more comfortably, and with generally less on the table, than could even the kook-iest of families, the Monkees, like the *Friends* they would become, sought to protect their environment from other generic incursions. Crucially, the mission of the friend-group sitcom was to resist turning into a *rom-com*. *The Monkees* succeeded, just about, but it's hard to think of another show that has done so in the six decades since.

The Liberation of Mary Tyler Moore

Apart from being two of the most popular sitcoms showcasing the corporate office as a space of women's liberation, the pilot episodes of *Who's the Boss?* and *The Mary Tyler Moore Show* share an odd feature: in both episodes, the central character responds ambivalently to apparent offers of sexual quid pro quo by men named Grant. It's a perfectly common name, and it's not impossible that the Grant beaten off by Angela Bower (Judith Light) in 1984 was named, consciously or unconsciously, after Lou Grant, the lovable, drunk curmudgeon played by Ed Asner in *The Mary Tyler Moore Show* between 1970 and 1977. But "Grant" still activates some of each episode's thematic treatment of the "woman question": verb and noun, allow and allowance; concede and concession; fund and funding. Mary and Angela's advancement is threatened, of course, by dimwitted colleagues with their brains in their dicks but also by an ambient sense that they are to be grateful for the positions that they have been offered, that their professional precarity is bound, in ways that they never fully understand, with their erotic lives. *Who's the Boss?* seems especially keen to stitch the girl-boss back into the domestic fabric of heterosexual social reproduction: though we are repeatedly informed that Angela is a powerful executive, most episodes take place within her domestic sphere, in which she squabbles on equal footing with her mother, lodger, and children. Even the show's title seems to undermine Angela's authority, as though the fact of a boss who was, in addition, a woman, has somehow unsettled the meaning of the word *boss*.

The later sitcom *Community* extracted a whole B plot from this little observational tidbit: the nerdy Abed Nadir (Danny Pudi) has been accepted into a competitive sitcom-watching class titled "Who Indeed? A Critical Analysis of Television's *Who's the Boss?*," taught by one Professor Peter Sheffield (Stephen Tobolowsky). While Abed insists that the answer is quite obvious—the boss is Angela, both in the office and in the home, where she employs Tony Micelli (Tony Danza)—Sheffield offers a set of increasingly panicked academic evasions, insisting that "the answer is not quite that simple, Mr. Abed. Few are." Later, Sheffield's defensiveness amounts to a ludicrous attempt to justify academic work on the sitcom by insisting, "I am not a fan. I am not a groupie. I am an academic. When I ask the question *Who's the Boss?*, it is a rhetorical question. When asked the question beyond the question, what is a boss?, that is even *more* rhetorical—" and so on. Eventually, Abed proves that Angela is the boss with a complex, mathematical diagram on the chalkboard, causing Sheffield to slump into his chair despondently, his life's work ruined. More than just a fable about the institutionalization of Angela's precarity by the patriarchal establishment Sheffield embodies, Abed's triumph reflects his greater access to digital archives, both of the show itself and of the interviews and other materials surrounding it—access that has vitiated the need for academics who boast of having had direct access to material archives. Abed's victory is less a triumph for feminist pessimism, then, and more an expression of techno-optimism, a belief that the pseudo-problems that humanists have upheld for generations can now be solved for good with just a search engine and a broadband connection.

Next to Angela's, Mary Richards's habitation of charismatic white womanhood appears unproblematically exuberant. The title sequence of *The Mary Tyler Moore Show* culminates in a cheerful Mary walking through metropolitan Minneapolis, pausing at a crossroads, and throwing her hat in the air, figuring thereby the new and independent life she is asserting as a productive worker, independent of marital or sexual contracts as a kind of commencement ceremony, as if her beanie were a mortarboard. Mary's decision to place sexual independence and clerical productivity (she goes to work as a producer for a local news program) above the marriage contract forms an ethical ground upon which the *Show*

attempts to stake out ground away from the heterosexual reproduction plot. Beginning a sitcom with a woman's belated decision
to break off an engagement and choose work instead positions the
sexually independent woman as an unusual kind of heterosexual
agent: Rachel Green (Jennifer Aniston) jilts her fiancé, Barry, in
the first episode of *Friends* but is quickly forced to pair up with the
drippy paleontologist Ross Geller (David Schwimmer); Jessica Day
(Zooey Deschanel) inaugurates *New Girl* by dumping her faithless
boyfriend, and she spends some time dating a series of dudes for a
few episodes at a time, but she, too, is eventually drawn into heterosexual social reproduction with the love of her life, Nick Miller
(Jake Johnson), whom she met after she dumped the douche. One
might observe this pattern and conclude that the gesture of establishing female sexual independence as a premise of a sitcom outside the home served merely as a device to subordinate the sitcom's
half-started/half-finished plot to a more forcefully teleological romantic comedy. Certainly, in *Friends*, arcs emerge at the scale of the
season and the series that do precisely that: the final episode concludes with Ross and Rachel finally paired up for good; Monica and
Chandler leaving Manhattan to live in their new house; and the
apartment space, in which romantic comedy and situation comedy
duked it out over ten seasons, is left in the darkness.

But the situation is a little more complicated with *The Mary Tyler Moore Show*. While the workplace is largely dominated by cari-
catures of men—at least until the appearance of Sue Ann Nivens
(Betty White) in season 4—the home setting features women:
Mary, her friend Rhoda Morgenstern (Valerie Harper), their neighbor Phyllis Lindstrom (Cloris Leachman), and Phyllis's daughter
Bess (Lisa Gerritsen). Mary herself is spared emplotment within a
romantic comedy, and the show ends with her and her colleagues
all being fired—a professional catastrophe, not a romantic one.
Rhoda and Phyllis have been positioned as incompatible rivals for
Mary's affection—Rhoda, traditional and worldly; Phyllis, a snooty
women's libber—which triangulation mimics *some* of the features
of a romantic comedy, in which multiple suitors are whittled down
through a series of ethical and aesthetic challenges.

But the bigger issue is the question of spin-offs. Mary is separated
from her best friend after season 4, when Rhoda returns to New

2.2 Mary Tyler Moore throws her hat in the air during the introductory sequence of *The Mary Tyler Moore Show*.

York, where her plot is structured as the antithesis of *The Mary Tyler Moore Show*: on the new show *Rhoda*, the protagonist falls for a man in the first episode, moves to New York in the second, and marries him in the eighth. By the third season, Rhoda and her husband, Joe Gerard (David Groh), had separated, and Rhoda was back in the marriage market, looking for another One. *Rhoda*'s conflicted relationship with romantic emplotment comes to a head in the third-season episode "Two Little Words ... Marriage Counselor," in which Joe and Rhoda go to a marriage counselor (played by a goading, antic René Auberjonois) and Joe admits, "I'm just not sure, but if I wanna be married, you're as good as I could get." The Rhoda/ Joe romantic plot ends by transforming Rhoda from a charismatic scofflaw into a whiny scold, who has to be punished for having "made [Joe] marry [her]." These developments were predictably unpopular with audiences, and *Rhoda* was canceled during its fifth season. A second spin-off, *Phyllis*, was launched the year after *Rhoda*, taking Phyllis and Bess (who gets a romance plot and is pregnant in the final episode) to San Francisco, leaving Mary with neither of her confidantes. In other words, the very threat of female sexual protagonism that emerges in the early seasons of *The Mary Tyler*

Moore Show between the three women is suppressed not through the introduction of a heterosexual romance but by the abduction of the two women whose affective bonds with Mary had sustained the show through its earlier seasons.

He's Her Lobster!

The transformative social project of heterosexuality, then, appears to be waging an unwinnable war against the body, in which sexual difference must be formulated again and again in the moments where its dissolution feels closest at hand, most undeniable. Enter the transsexual. Undeniably a creature of heterosexuality, the transsexual believes in sexual difference enough to embark on a project of sexual transformation but unmakes the conventional rubrics according to which the agent and reagent of heterosexuality might be designated. Every transsexual is, by definition, multiply sexed—as much the mannish woman as the effeminate man. The sitcom throws out (or up) figures of transsexual garishness not merely in the positions of Death Mommy and Doting Daddy but in the position where one would most anticipate sexual self-evidence: the position of the romancer. The inevitable product of this escalation, over time, is the emergence of what gets called *t4t* (trans for trans) intimacies, which is to say the non-ontologized settlement of transsexual suitors. We have swapped sex, back and forth, so many times, that any expression that commutes what is still called "gender" signifies nothing more keenly than its dialectical negation. Jessica Day (Zooey Deschanel) performs *ingenue* with such creamy bravado that we find ourselves drawn into speculations on her alto voice; her lover Nick Miller (Jake Johnson) is so shambolically macho that we check the size of his earlobes, notice the thinness of his facial scrub. The final phase of heterosexuality is its full, non-ontologizable transsexuality: Nick and Jess, April and Andy (and Ben and Leslie, for that matter), Marshall and Lily, Paul and Jamie, Mindy and Danny, Ned and Chuck, Louis and Jessica, Holly and Michael, Bob and Linda, Hank and Peggy.

Sitcom love is *t4t* love. Ergo:

(1) *Trans women don't get to escape heterosexuality.* Nobody does, but especially not one whose body has reconstituted itself as a heterosexual split screen. We *are* the mirror universe; we *are* the evil study group; we are *Sliders*. We are the "what if . . . ?" stories; the role play at weekends; the Reverse Flash; Bizarro; Zibarro; Hank Henshaw; Owlman. And we are narcissists: seeing ourselves nowhere, we feel ourselves everywhere, and we *identify*, constantly. We *identify* with Jessica Day, with Beverly Crusher, with Morticia Addams, with Sally Solomon. When the trans woman writes herself into the world, she does so under the sign of a heterosexuality whose contradictions have been intensified to the point of crisis. She is the scapegoat for heterosexuality but she is also its apotheosis, the ne plus ultra of heterosexuality, into whose event horizon heterosexuality is pulled, spaghettified. She is the Mao Tse-tung of "On Contradiction":

> The fundamental contradiction in the process of development of a thing and the essence of the process determined by this fundamental contradiction will not disappear until the process is completed; but in a lengthy process the conditions usually differ at each stage. The reason is that, although the nature of the fundamental contradiction in the process of development of a thing and the essence of the process remain unchanged, the fundamental contradiction becomes more and more intensified as it passes from one stage to another in the lengthy process. In addition, among the numerous major and minor contradictions which are determined or influenced by the fundamental contradiction, some become intensified, some are temporarily or partially resolved or mitigated, and some new ones emerge; hence the process is marked by stages. If people do not pay attention to the stages in the process of development of a thing, they cannot deal with its contradictions properly.[3]

Heterosexuality is, for feminists, the fundamental contradiction of social reproduction; its affective texture is the texture of inequity. And it is *desirable*: being fucked is desirable, though to say so invites concern and sometimes worse; being held in the long, strong arms ("they're American planes") of the maternal Daddy is desirable. Lord, make me chaste, but not yet: for Augustine, as for Mao, sexual difference is a phase in the epic of salvation. So the disciplinary notion that "it's just a phase" turns out to be true—not for the individual transsexual but for history as such. Capitalism is just a phase; patriarchy is just a phase; for the Freud of "Beyond the Pleasure Principle," the emergence of life from rock is merely a developmental phase. Contradiction subtends all and only looks like a phase from the perspective of universal heat death, which is not a position from which any archive, present or past, could be conceived.

(2) *Cis men who date trans women are heterosexual.* True, but the form of heterosexuality they practice can exist with the most viciously negated practices of masochism or (internalized) homophobia (is there any other kind?). Any ontology that presumes to resolve this contradiction ("trans women *are* women, cis men *are* men, therefore a relationship between trans women and cis men is heterosexual") abandons for mere simplicity the Hegelian insight that ontology is nonidentical with itself, that no syllogism can be sustained without a syntactical slippage between subject and predicate. The trans woman seeks non-ontology first and probably last—not because she wishes to be *not a man* rather than *a woman* but because the identity of the *woman* that she becomes is the principle of nonidentity cast in flesh. For this reason, the transsexual is the embodiment of heterosexuality—its only champion, its scapegoat. "He's her lobster": not merely is the lobster hermaphroditic; the two-toned lobster is hermaphroditic—the heterosexual dialectic given flesh and shell. For Ross and Rachel, it means that each will forever become the other, and neither will permit the other to freeze into being. If there is to be a spin-off (as there was), it would have to be retrieved from elsewhere (it was *Joey*).

The nonidentity of being and desire ("I am not what I wish") engrafts the subject of heterosexuality into the world, but even this dialectical logic is overturned by the collapse of being and desire in the queer scene—the position from which *to do* and *to be* appear at the same coordinates. The trans woman has no capacity, in fact, to accede to the ontological prompt ("what *are* you?"), since any utterance by which she would attempt to make herself known in response would have to begin by severing subject from predicate, in order to be seen to stitch them back together. In the utterance "I am a woman," for example, the subject only becomes a woman in

2.3 David Schwimmer and Jennifer Aniston kiss as Ross and Rachel in *Friends*. The subtitles underneath read, "See! He's her lobster."

the final word, up until which point she was only an "I." Nor could she give herself entirely to the negation of being in the name of desire, since desire will not restrict itself to the correct space of (non-) ontology. There is nothing to prevent us from desiring the impossible. We frequently do, and you can't stop us.

(3) *The meet-cute is the heterosexual clock.* I see you desiring my desire; you see me desiring your desire; we see each other desiring the nonidentity of our desires. Romantic comedy cannot escape ontologization: even at its most stubbornly noncommittal, it depends on making something out of nothing, making love out of nothing at all. (When Jim Steinman, who wrote those words, died, Meat Loaf said, "We didn't *know* each other. We *were* each other."[4] Meat Loaf died nine months later.) Something bigger than both of us: there is no comedy without the disciplinary threat of ontology; there is no love without being, as much as we might wish for it. The hard truth upon which trans femininity founders is that heterosexuality cannot be fully incorporated, either, but will always remain somewhat in and of the world, a system of governance rather than a practice of resistance. Strangely (or, conceivably, completely normally), the first major Hollywood rom-com starring a trans woman, *Together Together*, was neither a comedy nor, indeed, romantic: the film ends without any kind of romantic communication between Ed Helms

and Patti Harrison, despite the fact that Harrison's entire character is gestational heterosexuality—she's a surrogate. She's *his* surrogate, and props to the first out trans woman to get top billing in a Hollywood rom-com for signing on to a picture in which her entire character is cisness reduced to function, a brilliantly disillusioned heterosexuality even if a rather boring movie in other respects.

The situation comedy, we have seen, constitutes the heterosexual plot as incomplete, asymptotic, and repetitive. But the romantic comedy must be brutally teleological or it is nothing—such as philosophical movies like Richard Linklater's *Before* trilogy. The gradual subordination of situation comedy to romantic comedy, encapsulated by the cruel phrase *How I Met Your Mother*, marked its fundamental transformation, from the genre of heterosexual collapse to the genre of transsexual emergence. Not even as courageously fate-tempting a show as *How I Met Your Mother* can afford to forgo the closures upon which the episodic structure depends, hence the emergence of social frameworks in which romantic emplotment could be narrated in serial. The most obvious of these is the *serial monogamist*, whose routines seeped out from the small screen into the real world and now perhaps govern the social reproduction of heterosexuality more generally. The plurality of suitors is as old as the marriage plot: Portia's three suitors in *The Merchant of Venice* must choose between three caskets, of gold, silver, and lead. Freud traces this ruse to a medieval manuscript called the *Gesta Romanorum* and notes that, deathly and stuffable, "caskets are also women, symbols of what is essential in woman, and therefore of a woman herself—like coffers, boxes, cases, baskets, and so on." He concludes, inevitably, that a scene that had *appeared* to depict a young woman selecting a male suitor more fundamentally demonstrates that "the theme is a human one, *a man's choice between three women*."[5] Choice, in *The Merchant of Venice*, works both ways: Portia's choice is based on an evaluation of the suitors' choices. Nonetheless, Freud's thinking here, as often, turns to the transsexual logic at the core of heterosexuality, which, he has come to think, might simply be a failed or partial sublimation of a more primary transsexualism. In order to choose between Ross, Chandler, and Joey, Rachel Green (Jennifer Aniston), the protagonist, upon whose sexual independence *Friends* is founded, must make a choice like that of Shakespeare's

Portia: she must abstract her trio into categories and invert them, so that *their* choices can be evaluated. (Joey is gold: complexity melts in his radiance. Chandler is silver: he uses humor as a defense mechanism. Ross is lead: the fossil man, rained upon.) Freud goes on to suggest that the synchronic arrangements (the three caskets and Lear's three daughters) disguise diachronic schemes and that the choice really comes down to "the woman who bears him, the woman who is his mate and the woman who destroys him," where that last mother is "Mother Earth," to whom Freud also refers as "the silent Goddess of Death."[6] A problem with Freud's judgment is that it would clearly tend to privilege the second of the three as a sexual selection—not that he would object, since for Freud the second object is simply a replacement for the first, and the third (Death) is the only castration that actually befalls the one who believes himself to be choosing. Each of Freud's readings depends on a transsexual procedure, which appears in his text as casually as if a sex change were an inevitable effect of the syllogism as such: "Lear carries Cordelia's dead body on to the stage. Cordelia is Death. If we reverse the situation it becomes intelligible and familiar to us. She is the Death-goddess who, like the Valkyrie in German mythology, carries away the dead hero from the battlefield."[7]

Sitcom mothers rarely see themselves reproduced in sitcom suitors, if for no other reason than that the economy of serial television enumerates choices differently from five-act plays: the conceptual parsimony required to exhibit the items on stage at the same time requires that there be no more than three caskets, or three women, but in a ten-season show, dozens of lovers can be brought in, each to activate something slightly differently, moderately pathological, in the selecting subject—paradigmatically Rachel, but each of the others in due course too. Transsexuals embody heterosexuality but for that reason are barred from becoming heterosexuals. Meanwhile, heterosexuals are barred from noticing the degree to which their social position depends on the recognition of a provisional transsexuality, which they are forced to disavow in the practice of sex. Accordingly, the *Friends* don't amuse each other, and they don't amuse us directly, either: we don't laugh because Joey said something funny but because he said something *Joey*, so crisply typifying that the satisfaction of sexual selection can be restored without the cumbersome intervention of plot. The rom-sitcom therefore resurrects an aspect of traditional comedy that family sitcoms had neglected: wit. Yet where Portia or Petruchio use wit as both stick and carrot, in the rom-sitcom wit exists to clarify the differences between suitors: in that sense, their language is merely expressive and nonrelational, and *Friends* is the one thing that the six are most certainly not.

Capital and Cringe

We move from the family through the neighbor to the group of friends, and then finally into the workplace, where social relations are fixed by neither sexual nor ideological bonds but by whatever interests workers share by virtue of their position in the mode of production. In a well-known passage of *The German Ideology*, Marx and Engels describe the division of labor as it engenders a fundamental alienation of workers from various aspects of their inclinations. "For as soon as the distribution of labor comes into being," Marx writes, "each man has a particular, exclusive sphere of activity, which is forced upon him and from which he cannot escape." Accordingly, a person becomes "a hunter, a fisherman, a herdsman, or a critical critic, and must remain so," whereas in a Communist society, "society regulates the general production and thus makes it possible for me to do one thing today and another tomorrow, to hunt in the morning, fish in the afternoon, rear cattle in the evening, criticize after dinner, just as I have a mind, without ever becoming hunter, fisherman, herdsman, or critic."[8] In other words, where there was inclination, there is now identity: criticizing had been an aberration; the critic was now a species. What we might call a resistance to identity in Marx has its counterpart in Freud's thinking too, in the model of sexual repression that he develops in the "Three Essays on the Theory of Sexuality." In infancy, Freud tells us, we are bearers of a "polymorphous-perverse disposition" that can lead us "into all possible kinds of sexual irregularities."[9] Sexual development then proceeds by erecting "mental dams" to block such "sexual excesses" as are unwelcome or unbearable, and the phenomenon on the other side of maturation, our sexual orientation, is comprised only negatively, as whichever pleasure sources remain after the reaction formations ("shame, disgust, and morality") have had their say.[10] Freud, of course, does not imagine a future (Communist or otherwise) in which polymorphous perversity could be restored, but the model of individuation-by-selective-repression nonetheless echoes Marx's critique of the specialization imperative.

This convergence might help explain why it was in the final phase of the sitcom's withdrawal from the nuclear family—the workplace sitcom—as social bonds between characters weaken, the laugh track recedes, and appeals to realism are made by various parties, that nonetheless the intensity with which *character* is performed escalated hyperbolically. Ross, Chandler, and Joey all represent different types, but types of the same *genus* of object: sexually viable white New Yorker in his early thirties. Dwight Schrute, Jim Halpert, and Erin Hannon exemplify the differences of people whose only relation is the work relation, which is a nonrelation. As the sitcom slides into capitalist realism, it accordingly becomes all the less real and all the more extravagant. Even the most conspicuously embodied of performers in family sitcoms—Carolyn Jones's Morticia, say, or Lucille Ball—declines to spill as much sweat as Rainn Wilson squirts out in more or less every episode of *The Office*. Dwight's hyperactivity draws on the long tradition of sitcom zaniness, of course, but stripped of *I Love Lucy*'s executive force and lacking any of the sexual charisma or puerile exuberance of *The Monkees*. Rather, we are encouraged to see Dwight's extraordinary practices of embodiment as themselves a kind of capitalist literalism: he has decided to take corporate pablum like "assistant regional manager" at face value and live his life as though he were, indeed, assisting a man who was managing an entire region. It is not going too far to suggest that Dwight Schrute's body symptomatizes the contradictory relation between proletarian and bourgeois under neoliberalism, in which the worker is forced not merely to specialize (to become ever less a person and ever more a part of a person) but to recite the corporate garbage, sing the corporate anthems, and manifest the corporate affects whose logic has been designed not to illuminate the worker's condition but to annihilate everything *but* that condition.

2.4 Jim Halpert (John Krasinski) receives a cringe pan in *The Office*.

Clowning *as* capitalist realism. *The Office* began broadcasting in 2005, two years after the death of Charles Douglass, the inventor of the "audience response duplicator" (or "Laff Box"), which had become a scapegoat for genre fatigue aimed at the sitcom since its introduction in 1950; it was used to "sweeten" existing laughscapes from live audiences and sometimes to substitute entirely for laughter when none had appeared, either because the live audience was tired after multiple takes of the same joke or because the audience had departed before a scene could be shot. The Laff Box continues to serve as a reminder of the coercive dimensions of television and of genre more broadly: the television critic David Niven is quoted as having called it "the single greatest affront to public intelligence I know of."[11] The opening of an episode of *Cheers*, in which a member of the cast reports, "*Cheers* is filmed before a live studio audience," was widely interpreted as a guarantee of authenticity for any laughs heard during the show, as though the at-home audience could relax knowing that they weren't being cattle-prodded into merriment. Comedies didn't dispense with the laugh track at once—*How I Met Your Mother*, which debuted the same year as *The Office*, ran for nine seasons, with a laugh track and no studio audience whatsoever—but the longer-term success of the documentary-style comedy probably derives less from impatience with the sitcom as a mode of affective regulation (after all, why else would anyone watch them?) and more from the fact that *The Office* had developed a coercive tool more powerful than the laugh track: the cringe.

Like a compound sentence that ends with a disappointing pay-off, a cringe is a species of bathos, peculiar to the digital phase of comedy. That the term has generated unexpected psychological treatises, such as Melissa Dahl's spurious *Cringeworthy: A Theory of Awkwardness*, suggests a broader desire to internalize mediatic phenomena—that is, to treat popular cultural forms as though they arose organically from the experience of a perceiving subject. In a different way, as Charlie Markbreiter has argued, it is the tendency to take cringe as an, perhaps *the*, authentic aesthetic response to the alterity of phenomena that explains its weaponization against the self-expressions, especially, of trans people online.[12] The specificities of cringe nonetheless warrant closer scrutiny. Key to its deployment in *The Office* is its function as a reaction shot: Michael says something outrageous, and the camera seeks out the facial expression of Jim (or occasionally Pam, or even Oscar), who offers a raised eyebrow but little more, registering Michael's speech as a faux pas but declining to add any editorial observations. In a sense, this single-camera three-step (gaffe, pan, react) adds only an additional step to the traditional double-take reaction shot common to the multicamera setup since *I Love Lucy* (Lucille Ball and Desi Arnaz are often credited with having developed the three-camera sitcom reaction shot), in which the director could film both reactant and reactor at the same time and cut between them quickly. But the interposition of the middle step—the camera panning around to *find* Jim—marks a most significant development from the reaction shot. Laura Mulvey's famous theory of scopophilia presents the deployment of cutting away in classic Hollywood noir as a cinematic formalization of Freud's understanding of fetishism: in order to avoid gazing on the castrated body of his mother, which betokens his own castration, Freud's fetishist glances away—he cuts—to something else in his environs: his mother's feet (in which case he becomes a shoe fetishist) or her pubic hair (in which case he becomes a fur fetishist), and so on. Yet unlike the fetishistic cut, the cringe pan fails or refuses to reject the unseeable object entirely and instead dwells, if only for a second or two, in the unstable position of *attempting* to

2.5 Dwight Schrute (Rainn Wilson) looks at the camera in an episode of *The Office*.

find something worth fetishizing. So we could refer to the cringe pan as a kind of failed fetishism, in which the camera is not able to dispel the traumatizing effects of having seen the unseeable. The triumphant complicity that the cringe pan delivers, between Jim and the viewer, is nonetheless subject to a kind of shrinkage, as the pleasure that can be derived from excluding the abject being is contaminated by a trace of the abject that it had hoped to leave behind. The Jim Halpert cringe pan has endured in the form of so-called reaction GIFs: video clips of two seconds or less that can be used on social media to convey complex emotional responses to content nonlinguistically. To some extent, this usage is opportunistic: Jack Dorsey posted the first tweet on March 21, 2006, by which point *The Office* was reaching the end of its second season, and the cringe pan was already well established in the show's vocabulary. Yet notwithstanding the anachronism, the world of *The Office* is one in which character has already been reduced to a feed: a fully specialized perceiver and transmitter of affect, in whom the division of labor has engendered a completely isolated consciousness.

The Office remains positively utopian about what it thinks capitalism is, what we might call the ideological state apparatus of capital—its stories about itself; its institutionalization as a force for *reproduction*, outside of its governance of the mode of production;

"the American dream." Despite the ubiquitous cringing, or rather by virtue of the cringe's failure to detach itself from the object at which it is recoiling, it is impossible not to root for Michael Scott—for all his corruption, racism, and rapeyness, he is a scion of American capital every bit as salvageable as George Bailey. Tad Friend's description of Steve Carell's face in a 2010 *New Yorker* profile perfectly grasps the actor's midcentury grandeur: "Carell has a face built for comedy, its Sears-catalogue handsomeness hilarified by a butter pat of hair, an L-wrench nose, and deep-socketed, woe-is-me green eyes."[13] When Michael appeals to the camera, as he does often, he does so not in a spirit of social exclusion but from a desire to see and be seen. True recognition, for Michael as for Freud, depends on the consubstantiality of desire and aggression: "Would I rather be feared or loved? Easy. Both. I want people to be afraid of how much they love me." Even Jim, choking back his manly tears, delivers a monologue after realizing that Michael has plumped for an Irish exit: "And then tomorrow, I can tell you what a great boss you turned out to be. Best boss I ever had."

The fulcrum upon which *The Office* attempts to leverage a sentimental defense of the "best boss," without relinquishing its morbid analysis of "an American workplace," to give the show its original subtitle, is the distinction between the manager and the salesman. Forced to manage, Michael has gone doolally: he uses language as if mechanically because he has no idea—managers don't—of anything that is happening beyond the blinds of his little cell. The salesman, from Willy Loman to Shelley "the Machine" Levene, is a figure of charm, winsomeness, and pathos because he *knows* that he is misrepresenting the product he is slinging; he is therefore close enough to the production of commodities (or, in Levene's case, property deeds) that he shares the plight of the working man, even as he is forced by virtue of his position to forgo the comforts of solidarity and camaraderie that manual laborers enjoy. Michael's ambivalent desire for recognition from the warehouse staff, led by Darryl Philbin (Craig Robinson), racializes the form of belonging from which he exempts himself; nonetheless, his remarkable skill as a salesman remains one of the show's touchstones. When, in the fifth-season episode "New Boss," Michael quits, telling the CFO of Dunder Mifflin, "You have no idea how high I can fly," every character believes

2.6 As Michael Scott in *The Office*, Steve Carell stands on the roof of an office building.

that he is on a hiding to nothing, except for Pam, who dutifully follows him to the new Michael Scott Paper Company. They are joined by Ryan, Michael's erratic fuccboi mentee. When, a few episodes later, the inadvertent triumph of that solo venture allows him to walk back into the office and demand employment for himself and all his friends, his restitution enacts the final victory of sales against management. Even his gaffe is, for once, consummate: "How the turn . . . tables." Any potential for cringe is redirected into an act of true comic harmonization—the formal resolution of a real contradiction.

Walnuts

The *rom-sitcom* being not so much a subgenre as a retaliatory mechanism by which the sitcom preserves itself against the full articulation of its contradictions, it nonetheless engenders new relations to genre, centrifugally dispersed from the sitcom's nucleus, the blended family. We've seen the *workplace* and the *friends*; we can also observe the *showbiz sitcom* and, eventually, the introduction of *prestige*. The showbiz sitcom has nothing to do with the *Verfremdungseffekt*, Bertolt Brecht's optimistic notion that by displaying to audiences the mechanisms by which the culture industry does its business, that business might be interrupted, and spark for those watching a critical insight into the nature of representation under the capitalist mode of production. Indeed, the mythological *re*-enchantment of the scene of comic composition has been crucial to the ideologies of American comedy since they were devised, side by side with the sitcom, by Carl Reiner on *The Dick Van Dyke Show*, in the Friar's Club comedy roasts taking place in New York since 1950, and in the endlessly self-replicating cohorts of *Saturday Night Live*, which inhabits a curious position as an unofficial institutional licensor for US comics and comedy writers and is broadly supported with an enthusiasm fringed with pity. Central to these claims has been the figuration of the joke as an aesthetic device of infinite complexity and the joke writer as an arch technician, who adjusts the timing of his bits with the second-splitting skill of an artisanal watchmaker.

There's a line from the comedian Maria Bamford's 2017 Netflix special *Old Baby* that points to some of the complexities (of race, gender, violence, etc.) that this figuration has produced:

> It's not like I said I was Richard Pryor. And had I claimed to be one of the finest comedians of our past century, and been able to perform anything from his quintessential 1979 Long Beach stand-up special, or, perhaps, more weirdly, uh, been able to quote some of his lesser-known material about the difference between beating white women and black women. Uh, doesn't age well.

Bamford refers, in the knowing voice of somebody who expects her audience to be familiar with the same comedy arcana as she is, to Richard Pryor's well-established reputation as a genius whose off-stage mania was offset by the majesty of his onstage precision. Such a formalism, she shows, obscures the more obvious conformity of the offstage and the onstage: that Pryor's comedy itself sometimes consisted of narrative accounts of his violent antics. And yet Richard Pryor—a Black man who died in 2005—makes a convenient scapegoat for the idea of comedy as technical mastery that, of course, continues to nourish the comic careers of white sexual predators like Louis C.K. and bigots like Ricky Gervais.

The routine to which Maria Bamford refers, incidentally, appears as "Black and White Women," track 2 on the fourth disc of Richard Pryor's compilation album . . . *And It's Deep Too!* (2000). His violent assaults of women have been reported widely—in 1986, Jennifer Lee recounted in *People* magazine her experiences of physical abuse by Pryor: "I have the bruises and the hospital records to prove it."[14] These details underscore the essential *modernism* of American comedy—unsublimated rage figured as primitive insight, overlaid with a contrived, but never quite explicable, theory of technical expertise—Louis C.K. as Ezra Pound. And as with modernist poetry, the myth of (white) technical mastery founds itself by creating and incorporating an essentially anti-Black primitivism: playing the almost-eponymous character Tracy Jordan on *30 Rock*, for example, Tracy Morgan appears to provide a backdrop against which Tina Fey's Liz Lemon can cultivate her protagonism (fat, Black, and slow vs. thin, white, and fidgety). Latent and manifest content equals white technique and Black genius.

Yet *The Dick Van Dyke Show*, which began its run in 1961 and is cited as one of the earliest and most influential showbiz sitcoms, fits into this racially structured paradigm only uncomfortably. For one thing, Van Dyke was an extremely skilled physical actor who had spent six years touring a mime act called "The Merry Mutes," and from the credits onward, Carl Reiner's show delights in his elegance and physical charisma. Cary Grant may have been Walt Disney's preferred actor to play Bert in *Mary Poppins*, but the miscasting of Robert Preston in the 1957 opening of *The Music Man* wasn't set right until Dick Van Dyke took the role in the show's first revival in 1980. On screen, Van Dyke's physical presence resists the modern elements of his sitcom vehicle: his character, Rob, and his wife, Laura (played by Mary Tyler Moore), are often shown in separate beds watching television, and he works in a Manhattan skyscraper with two wise-cracking writers. But for all the midcentury New York fixings, Van Dyke skips through scenes like a butch Fred Astaire, seeming cheerfully out of place and even more delightedly anachronistic.

Indeed, depictions of anachronism, in which Rob Petrie is made aware of his being ill-fitted to his generic habitation, structure a remarkable number of the plots of *The Dick Van Dyke Show*. In one of the strangest, the second season's "It May Look Like a Walnut," anachronism prompts a genre panic that reaches an almost tidal intensity: for the longer part of the show's runtime, the audience is no more aware than Rob himself whether he is the victim of a practical joke being organized by Laura, whether he is dreaming, or whether he and everyone he knows have fallen under the control of a mysterious alien race from the planet "Twilo," whose apparent goal is to eradicate humans' thumbs and imagination by forcing them to eat special walnuts that they have dumped, en masse, on every set through which Rob moves; who "breathe" water (which they call "air"), and who have an additional set of eyes in the back of their heads. A reference to "the Twilo zone" establishes a generic debt to the sci-fi thriller anthology, then in its fourth season, and

2.7 Mary Tyler Moore, playing Laura Petrie in *The Dick Van Dyke Show*, surfs down a wave of walnuts.

Rob's paranoid interpretation of the walnut-filled world around him activates the familiar tropes of Cold War genre pictures—as does the appearance as the alien Kolak of Danny Thomas, the Lebanese American actor who had been the star of an earlier showbiz comedy named *Make Room for Daddy* since 1953, part of whose shtick involved playing up the ethnic ambiguity he signified for white audiences. The fetishistic dimensions of the paranoid fantasy—the eyes that gaze from behind full heads of hair, the threatened loss of thumbs and the associated loss of imagination, the ubiquity of nuts that everyone is trying to stuff in your mouth—therefore record more than merely a moment in American history during which audiences could not be expected to hear even the most clanging of Freudian alarms. They index the plastic, interactive relationship between body and environment, in which the meanings one can ascribe to bodies can become wholly rearranged in new generic contexts—a point underlined in the episode's extraordinary climax, in which Mary Tyler Moore literally swims through a tide of walnuts before smiling insouciantly at her uncomprehending husband.

The episode's genre play is less straightforward than it might seem. Rob's anxious inability to locate himself in genre is *itself* marked as a central element of a sci-fi thriller. That is, his very attempts to persuade himself that his life still makes sense as that of an urbane comedy writer disprove the contention, with the result that the audience loses its own generic certainty, and it begins to seem incomprehensibly plausible that, indeed, the Twiloites' bizarre walnut-based plot is not only the plot of the fictional movie, which Rob gleefully terrifies Laura by recounting, but it is also the plot of this episode of *The Dick Van Dyke Show*. The third possibility, that he was dreaming, turns out to have been true, but the revelation feels oddly belated and incomplete: after all, Rob had tested that theory several times in the episode, including by obtaining a punch to the face so that he could confirm that he felt pain. Easier to open up than to shut down, the paranoia of the sci-fi thriller thus exploits one of the generic particularities of the sitcom: that its very susceptibility to permeation by other genres leaves it relatively unable to establish its own ontological condition when called upon to do so. Perhaps Rob Petrie was dreaming, but Mary Tyler Moore really did the breaststroke through a cascade of thousands upon thousands of walnuts, in front of a live audience at Desilu Cahuenga Studios in Hollywood.

Please Tell Me That's the Name of Your Band

"Prestige sitcom" feels less like an oxymoron than a pleonasm: the promise of pleasure in any individual sitcom inheres in its minor differences from mere formulaic reproduction and therefore in its distinction. Nonetheless, it marks a historical shift in the distribution model of sitcoms in the genre's final phase: the migration of content onto online streaming subscription services. That migration pulled sitcoms into distribution networks according to which whole seasons were dropped on the same release date, which accelerated the decay of the already eroded discipline required to open up and close down a new plot within twenty-two minutes. Without schedules to balance or advertisers to solicit, episodes could stretch way past half an hour, and even hour-long episodes could stretch out into mini features: individual episodes of the supernatural thriller *Stranger Things*, which started off at between forty-two and fifty-six minutes in the first season, were running at between sixty-five and a hundred-plus by the fourth. And audiences were no longer expected to modulate their own viewing to a weekly rhythm: the term *binge-watching* seems to have been popularized around Netflix's release of three drama shows in 2013, but *BoJack Horseman*, which debuted the following year, explored the formal entailments of binge-watching more directly than others: the third-season episode "Love and/or Marriage," for example, ends with a character yelling "motherf!"; the following episode begins in the same location with the character completing the oath—"ucker!"

For a certain viewer, the term *prestige* designates not a class marker but a formal reassurance: this show will follow the travails of a talented but irascible white man, whose once-promising career has not quite played out in the way he'd hoped, as he follows an addiction down to the bottom of a deep well of lugubriousness. The apogean far point of this species of white "prestige" was *Breaking Bad*, which demonstrated that professionally disenchanted middle-aged white men are better at everything than anyone else, and if it weren't for affirmative action, they would be running everything from global chemical consortia to the Mexican meth cartel.[15] Racialization functions obliquely in the *BoJack* universe, where animals and humans coexist without much friction but where racial distinction reproduces difference across lines of species: Andre Braugher's performance as the exasperated rodent governor of California, Woodchuck (or "Woodcharles") Coodchuck-Berkowitz, draws on Braugher's popular performance as a police chief in *Brooklyn Nine-Nine*; the dolphin Sextina Aquafina (first played by Aisha Tyler, then Daniele Gaither) is likewise racially distinguished by her sartorial and vocal styles—a Black femme presentation of power, which infuriates and delights those in her orbit. Conversely, two of the leading characters—Diane Nguyen and Todd Chavez—are played by white voice actors, Alison Brie and Aaron Paul, a fact about which the show seems to develop an increasingly uneasy conscience as it progresses: Diana takes a trip to Vietnam to worry about her relation to her heritage, before writing a young adult novel about "Ivy Tran, Food Court Detective"; while Todd is eventually confronted by his darker-skinned stepfather Jorge (thereby revealing that Todd's biological parents were both white), who conveys his frustration that his stepson's whiteness has insulated him from the confounding social foreclosures to which he had been subject. Racial difference in *BoJack* is therefore superadded to species difference but may also be renegotiated in the performance.

Conscious of being the first new sitcom released by the season onto an online streaming platform—the unsuccessful but formally innovative fourth season of *Arrested Development* having been platformed the previous year—from the first episode *BoJack Horseman* delivers itself as a eulogy for the sitcom, interring the old genre and creating a new. The titular character was a sitcom actor, whose two shows, *Horsin' Around* and *The BoJack Horseman Show*, form the background to much of the plot: the first an optimistic 1990s blended-family show, the latter an edgy failure from 2007 that merged the mockumentary style of the moment with confrontational subject matter; neither BoJack Horseman nor *BoJack Horseman* seems remotely fond of these late-stage developments. The cheerful sitcom exemplified by *Horsin' Around*, while it has blocked BoJack's development by trapping him onscreen in a youthful form that never learns or grows and thus preventing any kind of decathexis or maturation once departed, remains an object of ambivalently sweet reminiscence for the show itself. The fictional show's theme song (released on Netflix as a standalone video) conveys the basic conceit:

> Three little orphans, one-two-three,
> without a home or a family tree
> until this horse said "live with me"
> and now we've got a new family.
>
> We're laughing and learning and loving a lot.
> Every new day is a dream.
>
> We were lost and now we're found
> and we're
> horsin' around.[16]

The poignancy of these words, especially when the horse who has told Todd to "live with me" seems incapable of laughing, learning, or loving, coexists with a sense of the serendipity encapsulated by *Horsin' Around*, the strange fact of unasked-for generosity in an orphaned world. *BoJack Horseman*'s creator, Raphael Bob-Waksberg, talks with warm condescension about the show's models: "I thought family sitcoms like *Full House, Growing Pains* and *Family Ties* were actually kind of powerful. There was something wonderful about their cheesiness and warmth."[17]

The care with which *BoJack* treats sitcom form, the better to revel in its abolition, appears nowhere more fully realized than in one of the episodes in which BoJack's conduct tips from *problematic* into *cancelation worthy*: the second-season episode "Escape from L.A.," in which the jaded actor (re "jaded," incidentally, I've wondered whether BoJack must be a horse because he is *jaded*, that is, "an inferior or worn-out horse") has run away to look up an old friend named Charlotte in New Mexico, stays with her and her family for a while, and ends up on the cusp of having sex with her daughter Penny before being thrown out of the house and returning despondently to town. From the episode's start, BoJack attempts to turn his stay with Charlotte and her family into a reverse *Horsin' Around* situation, where he might be accommodated into their domestic setting, becoming somehow its central figure without disrupting it. "So, I had another meeting today with the drama chair at SFCC—I think they're going to offer me a position!" he offers enthusiastically. And then: "There's a real stick-in-the-mud dean there, who doesn't like my in-your-face style. If I know me, it might lead to some pretty zany misadventures!" Yet the ploy has been doomed to fail since the start, and even the new sitcom premise reflects a retreat from BoJack's initial plan to establish a sitcom family with Charlotte of their own: he didn't learn that Charlotte was married with children until after arriving in Tesuque. After she tells BoJack she can't wait for him to meet "Kyle and the kids," a designation that he rather optimistically hopes is the name of a band, a new sitcom theme plays in the style of the *Horsin' Around* song:

Kyle and the kids!
Kyle's the dad and Charlotte's married to him,

and they've got some kids:
there's Penny, she's going to high school;
she's got a brother; the brother's name is Trip.
They're the perfect family.
Kyle and the kids!
He loves his wife, and there's nothing you can do
Kyle and the kids—
nothing's going to be all right,
be all right, oh no.

Sitcom form then becomes a vehicle for a cynical irony, where Bo-
Jack's fantasy of finding belonging with an old flame slots him into
the self-sufficient "perfect family" in which his presence can only
be felt as the very opposite of belonging.

Yet while a pastiche of a sitcom theme clues the audience in
to the horrors to follow, "Escape from L.A." develops not so much
as a sitcom episode but as a disturbing and anachronistic species
of procedural. About halfway through the episode, BoJack invites
himself to Penny's high school prom—a questionable but passable
plotline for a sitcom but also a possible premise for an episode of
Law & Order: SVU—and the audience is handed a set of clues that
position the coming denouement as an ethically complex type of
case. We learn that, unlike her friends, Penny hasn't drunk any al-
cohol, that she is frustrated at her family's reluctance to take her
maturity seriously, that she is above the legal age of consent in
New Mexico—each of these details dropped into the dialogue with
the same conspicuousness as the "Kyle and the Kids" theme. The
sitcom-as-horror depicted in that quick song presents a world of
immobilization and entrapment, but the procedural develops mo-
mentum in the direction of something even worse—a traumatizing
event from which perspective mere stagnation feels like a lost bliss.
As that event (whose details are, of course, unknown until they are
not) pushes ever closer to the present, BoJack makes a needy and
joyless pass at Charlotte, softly and ambiguously rejects one from
Penny, and then leaves his door open, such that sometime later
Charlotte, and the viewer, burst through the now-closed door to
find BoJack and Penny fumbling with each other's clothes on his
bed. The focal point now positioned behind BoJack and Penny, we

2.8 In a still from *BoJack Horseman*, a deer, her human father, and her human brother smile at the camera. The text on the screen reads, "KYLE AND THE KIDS."

watch Charlotte standing aghast in the doorway, an inversion of the primal scene: mother as horrified spectator to the sexual convergence of daughter and interloper. This scene, however, cannot *literally* be "primal" for the same reason that BoJack's life cannot be a sitcom: he is expendable, and whatever wounds he has opened will be treated first and foremost by kicking him out of the family home, and of "Kyle and the Kids," for good.

The sophistication with which *BoJack Horseman* exposes the limitations of sitcoms to achieve even the type of closure for which we (or BoJack) might turn to them has been, justifiably, a major feature of the many critical plaudits that the show's creators, Bob-Waksberg and Lisa Hanawalt, received. Less noticed has been an element of the show that is more distinctly the animator Hanawalt's creation than Bob-Waksberg's: the erotic delight in animal flesh that the show's visual style activates—a bright golden retriever in a V-neck tee; a thick-thighed pug; a vain and manipulative rabbit, combing his ears with the mannerisms of an early 1960s closet case. In that sense, *BoJack* belongs to another oblique contemporaneity: the time of *furries*, and of the animal avatars whose playful projection or inhabitation grounds their sexual and social relations. Masterful in its dismantling of genre, *BoJack* is therefore even more impressively unmasterful in its mediation of sexual affect, whose splurges of intensity manifest as blotches of ink on bodies, unconstricted by either sitcom sameness or procedural damage.

No Scar

The remarkable economy of the sitcom, which opens and closes a plot within twenty-two minutes, tests the limits of the dramatic framework from which it has acquired its operative theory of brevity: the nineteenth century's "well-made play." Desi and Lucy have picked it up, sure, through Hollywood melodrama, which in turn drew on Eugene O'Neill and the Barrymores, but the authors and theorists were Henrik Ibsen, Oscar Wilde, and Anton Chekhov. Lynn Spigel shows how early sitcoms moved *away from*, rather than toward, vaudeville and variety.[18] The most famous principle of well-made drama was formulated by Chekhov: "one must never put a loaded rifle on the stage if it isn't going to go off. It's wrong to make promises you don't mean to keep."[19] The parable of Chekhov's gun disguises as an ethical principle what is at core a strong dualistic claim about the nature of representation. As was obvious to Ernest Hemingway, the unfired (or, in his word, "unfireable") gun makes just as powerful a symbol as a fired one: arrested in latency by "a good enough writer," the gun can be removed from the economy of mere plot and elevated to a psychological detail—or, rather, a sexual detail, since one would have to admit that Hemingway's pair of explanations—"maybe he is queer for guns, or maybe an interior decorator put it there"—eroticizes the unfired gun with an unexpected Twinkie defense.[20] Indeed, the unfired gun is better, since a gun furnishes a space queerly *only* if it is allowed to remain cocked but unshot: latency as tumescence, the *enceinte*. Chekhov's gradual transformation of latent material into a plot indexed by the *shape* of that material aligns his thriftier dramaturgy with the aspect of sitcom form I have been calling "formulaic." Guns go off (of course), but pipes are there to be smoked; rosebuds are there to be cut; eggs are there to be protected and then (perhaps) to crack open in the same way as a baby's skull. As we have seen, the sitcom exists in order to unfurl the narrative and logical implications of one etic element at a time, to show how a pipe, or an egg, or a gun, or a dishwasher can pressurize the prevailing premises of a given show but then relent, such that those premises remain ductile enough to be challenged again. The premise *itself* is an unshot gun: perhaps, in another world, a postheterosexual tomorrow might have been clicked into being by the sheer illocutionary force of an utterance. But language never appears at risk of going off; it just smears queerness into every space, never pulling the trigger.

Queerness, if one could risk an epigram, is the confusion between a desire and an identity; paradigmatically, the form of objective misrecognition that prompts one to wonder whether one is treating the other as an idealized erotic object or as an alienated ego ideal. *I didn't know if I wanted to do him or to be him.* If queerness is not the exclusive preserve of homosexuals, as queer theorists have often insisted, that would be at least in part because heterosexuality is powerless to resist queer anticipations: indeed, heterosexuality in the strong sense is impossible, since in order to be recognizable as an erotic object, an object must possess some element of relational sameness, if only in the way that a raven is like a writing desk. Homosexuality, perhaps, would seem impossible on the same grounds, except that the word *homosexual* accelerates this very contradiction through a syntactic device: *homo*, for sameness, meet *sexual*, for difference. A gun that is fired moves sharply from latency to action, from identity to desire: it can't bespeak a "jerk" who's "queer for guns" until it recedes from plot again, becoming a gun that has been fired, ceasing to be a gun that is fired.

The conversion of various apparently singular objects into plot consistently structured the sitcom, but the excuse for this excursus is only that Chekhov's parable of the gun may itself sketch out the master plot of heterosexuality, in which case the final mutation of the sitcom would not be *BoJack Horseman*, a show that, after all, fires the many guns it parades through its six seasons, but a show that debuted a decade prior: *Arrested Development*. The title, elegantly enough, conjoins two of the setting's most important elements: the fact that the Bluth family is a construction firm (hence, development) and the fact that none of the spoiled rich Bluth kids ever quite managed to cut their way out of their mother's apron strings (hence, arrested). Yet "arrested development" might also describe the show's truly unusual, and virtuosic, method, according to which almost no joke is made a single time, and each time a character delivers a laugh line that none of them have said before, the viewer can be fairly sure that every single major character will say it, or some version of it, before the end of the third season. Is this pattern a going-off gun or a queer-for-guns gun? Its's the former, because each new object handled by *Arrested Development* will recur and will have accumulated more meaning and history in the meantime. It's also the latter, because at a different ordinal scale, the multitudinous repetition of jokes deprives each one of them of the kind of narrative pulsion that Chekhov aimed for. *Arrested Development* articulates a relation to form in which it is accurate to say *both* that the gun goes off *and* that it does not go off—a relation to form in which heterosexual social reproduction is tantalizingly indistinguishable from its dialectical, queer subversion.

One of the most densely woven of these running jokes concerns the relationship between Buster Bluth (Tony Hale), the sheltered mommy's boy, and his overbearing mother, Lucille Bluth (Jessica Walter). Buster's mother love draws him into a romantic entanglement with his mother's rival, Lucille Austero (Liza Minelli), who is generally referred to as "Lucille Two." The homophone of "Lucille too" underscores the point that Buster's attraction to Lucille Two is more properly a displaced attachment to his mother too. The verbal oscillations occasioned by the presence of two Lucilles amplifies over the course of the second and third seasons, most dramatically when Buster's hand is bitten off by a "loose seal," a seal who was released after an abortive "seal deal" that another character realizes she has neglected at the moment when she is invited to "seal the deal"—that is, to consummate a marriage to Buster's older brother George Oscar Bluth (Will Arnett), or "Gob," pronounced like the prophet Job. In a rather straightforward sense, the "loose seal" has become another agent of Buster's mother's castrating affection; in a slightly more complicated one, the seal is an avatar of his *brother's* sexual dysfunction and generalized impotence, the author of which (we are shown many times) was not Lucille but her husband, Gob's father, George Bluth (Jeffrey Tambor). More mitotic doublings and divisions ensue: George gave his eldest son his own name and that of his identical twin brother, Oscar. *Arrested Development* develops as an arrested semiotic system endlessly churning the same few elements, whether in the form of names—George's second son, Michael Bluth (Jason Bateman), gives his own son the name "George Michael," played by Michael Cera. Even the psychological implications of the doublings—or in the form of catchphrases, like the "I'm a monster!" that Buster develops after losing his arm—are deployed over and again. In the belated follow-up season 4, produced and bundled by Netflix seven years after Fox canceled the original, the writer Mitchell Hurwitz takes the idea even further, narrating the same scenes again and again from the perspectives of each of the different characters, demonstrating that, even when they thought they were running away from each other, they were in fact flying on the same plane, in disguise at the same party, and so forth. The plot of the fourth season is inferred through the spatial superposition of each of the episodes—an ambitious (and mostly panned) attempt to spatialize narrative in the same way that the show had always repeated jokes.

Incestuous love seems, often, positioned as the referent of the running jokes—that which can't be uttered and has therefore become a definitive feature of *everything* that is uttered. George Michael's attraction to his cousin Mae "Maeby" Fünke (Alia Shawkat) governs much of his emplotment—even her name seems to suggest a titillating but anxiogenic come-on. (Confusions over Maeby's age, as an index of her sexual viability and professional status, is another running joke—an uncomfortable one, since it seems partly to be an appeal to the viewer on behalf of a young teenager.) Buster's attachment to Lucille One remains the source of most of his physical and emotional needs over the show's duration. Even Michael, the closest thing the show has to a straight guy, develops a crush on a woman he believes (falsely, as it turns out) to be his older sister—a character played by Jason Bateman's own sister, Justine Bateman—and then his actual sister, Lindsay Bluth Fünke (Portia de Rossi). Incest emerges as the herald of heterosexuality's negation, its formal sign the running joke, according to which not merely are external elements converted into sameness but the like objects themselves proceed by converging, in ever more fraught ways, with each other.

But there's more to the Bluths than incest. Increasingly through-out the first three seasons, a presence makes itself felt behind the virtuosic patterning, which wants to designate itself as a "political" species of meaning. Its first appearance can be traced to the first-season episode "Let 'Em Eat Cake," in which George, who has been jailed awaiting trial for financial mismanagement of the Bluth Company, confesses to Michael that he "may have committed some light treason" by developing properties in Iraq. During the three years in which the show ran, between 2003 and 2006, the American-led invasion of Iraq, according to the World Health Organization, caused the death of 151,000 Iraqi citizens; none of his supposed "weapons of mass destruction" had been retrieved by occupying forces, and Saddam Hussein had been arrested and compelled to stand trial in Iraq for crimes against humanity, for which he was convicted and executed late in 2006. The penultimate episode of the third season of *Arrested Development* ties up what remains of the "light treason" plot through an odd series of coincidences: Michael has found a "secret room" in his house and has learned that Saddam Hussein's family and lookalikes lived in a house identical to his; he travels to Iraq, inspects one of the houses, meets Saddam's lookalikes who live there, checks in the secret room in the Iraqi house, and discovers what looks like what the former soldier Buster recognizes as "a mid-range nuclear warhead." Upon closer inspection, however, Michael notices that the warhead is "a Homefill," meaning "the company that makes the fake stuff we fill the model homes with." Inside the homefill warhead is a recording device, placed by the CIA, revealing that George Bluth had in fact built the model home in Iraq in order to surveil the lookalikes. George Bluth's name, we belatedly realize, seems to have been a light encryption of "George Bush"—who was *himself* a duplicate, named after his father, who also invaded Iraq. (Even Bush Sr.'s invasion of Iraq replicated, in the sense described by Avital Ronell in her essay "Support Our Tropes: Reading Desert Storm," his own father's more storied war record—Prescott Bush had served as a field artillery captain in World War I.)

This gonzo pileup of simulacra, lookalikes, model homes, home-fill, namesakes, and bullshit, all in the service of American imperial power, culminates in Gob and Michael watching embedded foot-

2.9 On a small TV glimpsed in *Arrested Development*, a Saddam Hussein impersonator speaks in a courtroom.

age of Saddam Hussein on trial, apparently protesting that he is a lookalike and not the real Saddam at all: "the real Saddam has a scar on his head; I'm no scar, I'm no scar, dot-com."

The words attributed to Saddam echo a website erected by Oscar Bluth (also Jeffrey Tambor) after his twin brother, George, swapped places with him and sent him to prison in his place, "I'm Oscar dot-com." The alignment of the lookalike with the identical twin is, in one sense, merely the latest of these matching games that *Arrested Development* has been playing since the start. In another sense, by extending the George Bluth–George Bush analogy to include Saddam Hussein and, implicitly, the cardboard weapons of mass destruction that the Americans have sold him, *Arrested Development* ends by affirming the notion of post-9/11 American foreign policy as part of a "civil war," as Michael Hardt and Antonio Negri put it. Yet putting these words in the mouth of a prisoner of war, whose trial is being watched on television—as if he were screaming from behind the glass—finally ruptures the diegetic self-sufficiency that *Arrested Development* had been modeling. Someone is trying to tell us something—perhaps language itself is trying to tell us something, as Georges Perec put it—something that might explain the fundamental nature of power. This spectacle of an incarcerated man—a racialized figure who was killed by the Iraqi client state less than a year after the episode first broadcast—necessitates, for the show as well as for the viewer, a radical closure on a scale larger and more terrible than even heterosexuality.

EPILOGUE
PARAL-
LELS

On Knowing a Body

While the sitcom recedes, the procedural—a genre at least as old (*Dragnet* debuted in 1951)—seems to be going stronger than ever. The term designates an episodic structure, in which a returning cast of characters investigates and solves a new case and therefore groups together types of dramas that viewers may be more inclined to treat as relatively distinct: viewers of medical procedurals are not necessarily equally partial to police procedurals; political procedurals like the early seasons of *The West Wing* address different audiences than veterinary mysteries. Still, a "procedure" is something more than a plot: the term implies not merely a procession of events but the protocols under which events process and implicitly also the institutional governance of those protocols within whatever setting they are progressing. We can therefore distinguish the procedural from the "golden age" whodunnits of Agatha Christie, Dorothy L. Sayers and others since their dashing detectives rarely operated on behalf of, or within, institutions, so that although Poirot may have treated Inspector Japp with a distant disdain, he was never obliged to slam a badge on his desk and tell him *he* was out of order. (We see little of his years in the Brussels police force.) The whodunnit celebrates the intuitive intellect of a gentleman uncaptured by bourgeois institutionalization; the procedural details the collaborative, albeit often also coercive and repressive, work of an institutional framework. In his descriptions of "America's wound culture," Mark Seltzer draws connections between the obsessive textuality of the detective and that of the serial killer.[1] The procedural therefore belongs to the broader generic history of "case study," as scholars have described it: in Lauren Berlant's terms, a "case represents a problem-event that has animated some kind of judgment."[2] Berlant goes on to suggest that the case study has developed as a biopolitical device for converting singularity into generalizability, and it thereby resolves the scalar problems intrinsic to any field of knowledge in which the character or meaning of a whole is derived from the examination of one or some of its parts. Procedurals yield only fictional knowledge—in that sense, analogous to the anecdote in Joel Fineman's accounts of it—but they yield such knowledge nonetheless.

The presumptive object of procedural knowledge is a body, just as the presumptive object of sitcom knowledge is a family. Procedures induce narrative from a body, such that a synchronic object—a corpse, or even a patient in so far as that patient is codified in a case history and a set of tests—can be followed upstream into the catalytic event from whose causal nexus the object has been ejected. Reflecting on the philosophical condition of the event, Michel Foucault writes:

> The event is not of the order of bodies. And yet it is not something immaterial either; it is always at the level of materiality that it takes effect, that it is effect; it has its locus and it consists in the relation, the coexistence, the dispersion, the overlapping, the accumulation, and the selection of material elements. It is not the act or the property of a body; it is produced as an effect of, and within, a dispersion of matter. Let us say that the philosophy of the event should move in the at first sight paradoxical direction of a materialism of the incorporeal.[3]

The event toward which a procedural advances both is and is not a material object: the body, accordingly, figures as both the grounding metaphor of materiality and a legible sign in its own right. The image of "a materialism of the incorporeal" recalls the theory of optography in early crime fiction—the belief that the last image a person sees before they die is emblazoned on their retina, the corpse as camera. The narrator of Auguste de Villiers de L'Isle-Adam's 1867 novella *Claire Lenoir* perceives a monstrous vampiric creature "lift[ing] with one hand, towards the abyss, a bloody head, with dripping hair."[4] Though real bodies, of course, do not retain material traces of virtual images, which they cannot reconstruct except by confabulation, nineteenth-century dreams of a perfectible, mechanical body endowed procedurals with one of the genre's grounding metaphors: the keen, trained perceptual apparatus of the investigator, whose intellectual magnificence, undimmed by institutionalization, rivals those of his free-range counterparts in the private detection game.

Across a range of genres and adaptations, Sherlock Holmes has been sorted into both camps at different times: Basil Rathbone's Holmes is as disaffected a mandarin as David Suchet's Poirot, but Johnny Lee Miller's Holmes works for the early twenty-first-century New York Police Department, and the show in which he appears, *Elementary*, is in most respects a conventional procedural. Benedict Cumberbatch's *Sherlock* exhibits elements of both gritty procedural antihero and dandy detective. (In an insightful essay drawing connections between Oscar Wilde and Raymond Chandler, Len Gutkin explores the strangely gendered figure of what he calls "the dandified dick."[5]) Hugh Laurie's performance as Gregory House in the medical procedural *House, M.D.* presents an unusual remediation: whereas usually Holmes's detection depends on a capacity for reanimation, for extracting a narrative from a (dead) body, House's particular genius is to catch the villain (the diagnosable illness) using a series of clues (symptoms) *before* the carrier of those symptoms becomes inert. House wears his debt to Holmes only opportunistically—his confidante is not John Watson but James Wilson, who gives him a copy of Joseph Bell's *A Manual of the Operations of Surgery* for Christmas one year; his drug of choice is Vicodin rather than cocaine; and his instrument is piano rather than violin—but his appearance as a diagnostician nonetheless illuminates the possibility of reanimating the backstory of a *living* organism rather than confabulating a prehistory of the dead. House's catchphrase, "everybody lies," conveys a desire not to discover a preexisting truth but to change a preexisting story. His patients, or cases, conventionally discover that their stories about themselves are fictions because they have been forced to swallow other people's lies or they have come to internalize their own. Not a few discover that their bodies are not sexed as they had believed. House's *narrative* surgery therefore positions him between detective and analyst: his treatment is complete not merely when a diagnosis has been reached (however much he professes merely to enjoy puzzles) but when the patient has been forced to confront, and can thereafter avow, the trivializing fictions with which they have been defended against acceptance of their true nature.

In certain respects, *House, M.D.* muddles the distinction between sitcom and procedural: for one thing, it's funny, though the madcap antics of an unstable genius trampling on liberal niceties likely hit a little different after 2016. For another, the show carefully crafts B stories into each episode, focusing on the rudiments of private life accorded to House's medical support staff. As might be the case in a sitcom, the B stories rarely advance; they merely accrue details: Taub is a philanderer; Kutner is an orphan; Thirteen is a bisexual woman with Huntingdon's chorea. However, the show's fourth season, distinctively, delivers a narrative arc, which confronts the implications of "everybody lies," approaching as if by a Freudian detour the question of transsexuality and sexual transition raised by House's practice. Having lost all three of his junior doctors at the end of the third season, House recruits forty interns to compete against each other for three fellowship positions; one by one they are eliminated until a midseason finale in which a philander, an orphan, and a bisexual successfully oust "cutthroat bitch" (CTB), whom House deems a capable physician whose abrasive and ambitious personality rules her out of longer-term employment. A few episodes later, House learns that his beloved confidant, Wilson, has started dating CTB, whose name is "Amber." Compulsively fascinated by his friend's choice of lover, House eventually determines that Amber's personality qualifies her to serve Wilson as an effective sex-swapped proxy for himself: that is, he realizes that he too is a "cutthroat bitch," or he would be, if he hadn't been a man. Increasingly self-impressed at his largesse in allowing Wilson to pur-

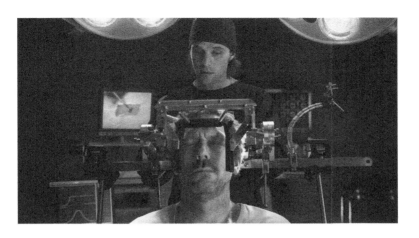

E.1 Hugh Laurie as Dr. House lies inside a medical contraption in *House, M.D.* Chase, played by Jesse Spencer, stands behind him.

sue a relationship with Amber and gratified by the autogynephilic pleasure he can derive from picturing a feminine version of himself, House enjoys squabbling with Amber over "custody" of Wilson, and the three of them converge to form a blended family of a sort not wholly remote from a sitcom. In the climactic two-part season finale, House is forced to confront the limits of his own cross-sex identification when he is in a bus crash and loses his memory, recovering it piece by piece until he realizes that he was seated next to Amber at the moment the bus crashed; moreover, he recalls that at the exact moment of the crash, he realized that she was exhibiting a symptom that, if untreated, would kill her—but he doesn't remember the symptom or the implied diagnosis. In order to obtain this memory, in an act of service to Wilson, House allows the handsome junior doctor Chase to perform "deep brain stimulation," probing his deep brain tissue with a sparking electrode, in hopes of recovering the memory. The season-long troping into cerebral feminization by transsexual identification therefore culminates in an image of House, head open, getting fucked in the brain by a beautiful blonde twink, in order to retrieve the version of himself that his lover could love, that could have been lovable, either to Wilson or to himself. The process succeeds in restoring the memory—Amber had been taking flu meds when the bus crashed, leading to kidney damage and therefore blood poisoning from the meds—but does not succeed in saving Amber, who is woken up in order to say goodbye to Wilson and the team but not House, who in addition to having lost the object of his identification has now also lost any of the love that his friend *could* have borne him. Things get patched up next season, of course, as they would in a sitcom, but it is too late for *House, M.D.* to renounce the knowledge of its own material being that the fourth season delivered at melodramatic pitch: in a drug-fueled hallucination of Amber at the end of the fifth season, his ghostly femme doppelganger tells him, "This is the story you made up about who you are." Everybody lies—even the body itself.

Nobody Exists on Purpose

Writing about comedy can be a bleak experience. Freud's book *Jokes and Their Relation to the Unconscious* makes for notoriously sober reading: it's funny, in a perverse sort of way, to watch an Austrian physician struggle, and ultimately fail, to recount and then neutralize every single joke he can think of. Dismantling pleasures, especially such pleasures as are taken in cruelty, can be a necessary as well as entertaining critical practice and has been theorized especially sharply by feminist cultural critics like Laura Mulvey and Sara Ahmed.[6] But the works I've been describing here contain jokes and mirth of many different sorts, not all so obviously sadistic as those against which Mulvey writes, and so the smashy-smashy type of criticism wouldn't really have worked and may have ended up as dull to read as Freud's book. To write about comedy is to grapple with an object that is very frequently sought out, and sometimes even obtained, from the culture industry. It takes many forms: pleasure, relief, joy, comfort, solace, companionship, the agreeable fantasy that the world is salvageable, compensation for the violence one experiences in one's life, hope. Whether or not one believes that people *should* seek these things out, or whether one personally gets anything out of any given sitcom, or any given episode, or joke, to write seriously about comedy is to forgo for however long one's *own* investments of this kind.

I found myself watching sitcoms for hours and hours on end during grad school. It was procrastination, interrupted by bouts of hard drinking and masturbation. Days, weeks, months—surely not years?—could pass in which I had done little more than watch a season of *The Mindy Project*, a show I have never especially enjoyed. It was procrastination but of a peculiar type: like alcoholism, the compulsive consumption of television can feel like service to an occult deity—a kind of daily ritual practice that can take up the larger part of one's waking hours, processing plot and feeling its oscillations stirring characters (and me) mildly out of their "comfort zones" and then back into them. The practice recurred during the COVID lockdowns. Days, weeks, months—honestly, most of 2020–21—were spent in or near my bed. I caught COVID myself three times and am still dealing with postviral brain-fog symptoms (writing seems to be about the only thing I can focus attention on for more than a few minutes at a time)—and so sitcoms returned, servicing the algorithm, educating the machine learners how to market to me and by extension to the class fraction to which I belong. If you're not paying for it, you're what's being sold. Et cetera. At a certain point, this mechanical practice had become work from which any pleasure had been rigorously expunged. I laugh so infrequently at television that when I did so recently—at Michael Sheen's delivery of the line "the poet Ovid mused, the wrong is merely the tail of the same beast as right" in *The Spoils of Babylon*—I stopped watching immediately and called my husband over to discuss it with him. I find the line funny because I can't figure it out, I suppose. It's more than the sum of its parts: Sheen's smugly knowing smile; the mock erudition of the Ovid reference; the garbled introduction of a *beast* into an otherwise banal statement of moral relativism ... Even my involuntary laughter, though, felt academic, as though chancing upon a rare specimen in the wild.

In the week when I was compiling this material and finalizing its shape, a young man broke into an elementary school in Uvalde, Texas, murdered twenty-one people, mostly young children, with an AR-15 assault rifle, and seriously wounded another seventeen.[7] How to talk about it? Thinking about comedy—and thinking, as I have come to, that comedy provides a useful rubric for thinking

through the specificities of American modernity, the violence traf-
ficked under the sign of that nation, its catastrophically uninter-
rogated capacity for unseriousness—seems grotesque, trivializing,
inhuman. Lily tells me of the sadness she feels at the foundational
and relentless violence of American history, and that she's a little
too annoyed about it to think of it as farce. Which isn't to say that
she doesn't appreciate the dark humor of the moment. She suggests
we take shooting lessons together when I visit her in Michigan later
this week. I feel sure that no part of the Uvalde massacre, from the
argument between Salvador Rolando Ramos and his grandmother,
to the cops advising kids to shout so that they could be located, to
the mutilated bodies of children, to an ancient president's appeal to
the apparently commonsensical proposition that "deer aren't running through the forest with Kevlar vests on, for God's sake. It's
just sick"—no part of this is tragic. Even the sickening regularity
of this kind of occurrence depends on an unpardonable comedy:
the comedy of the Comedian in *Watchmen* and the Joker in *Batman*.
After a brief disturbance, the organism reverts to the homeostasis
that generated the stimulation: one hormone responds "thoughts
and prayers," while its control hormone also says "thoughts and
prayers," in a slightly different voice.

Which is to say, comedy has become the genre by which horror
makes itself known to the world. Respectable broadsheets carry editorials about pornography; pro-ana sites, many of which were successfully suppressed after a moral panic between the 1990s and the
early 2010s, no longer seem to provoke the same terror they used
to; and the genre of white inexpressivity that once generated editorials condemning "industrial metal" lost, although Marilyn Man-
son's heel turn generates a kind of nostalgia. On the other hand, the
shock-comedy websites of the late 1990s and early 2000s, like rot-
ten.com, ogrish, and meatspin, mutated into larger general-interest
message boards like 4chan, 8chan, and KiwiFarms. These digital
ecosystems are distinct, and each is more politically diverse than is
generally credited, but a common element in these message boards
is the nihilistic mode of comic reasoning known as "blackpilling."
Unlike the term *redpill*, which is used online to denote antifeminist
consciousness raising among conservative men (and sometimes
women), the blackpill is the more politically ambivalent sign of a

E.2 The black-and-white trollface meme by Carlos Ramirez, with text reading, "U MAD BRO?"

terminally pessimistic, cosmologically cynical defeatism. Laughter, while it may not be morally redemptive or even aesthetically desirable, nonetheless functions within blackpill discourse as a kind of sustaining, rather than nourishing, caloric currency. On Kiwi-Farms, the "libs" and "troons" (trans people) singled out for mockery and contempt are known collectively as "lolcows"—livestock "farmed" for whatever chuckles they can yield. The blackpill worldview claims a kind of libertarian political independence, but of course even the investment in a species of laughter indistinguishable from cruelty, whose heroes are Louis C.K. and Dave Chappelle, governs the unmistakable political aesthetics of American fascism. This emerging sense of the comic as a stubborn refusal to budge—nothing more or less than a mobilization of that fascist anthem "Won't Back Down"—but from the position of male abjection, the masculinity of the basement-dwelling incel, who takes a manic delight in the discomfort one provokes in others. The desire takes iconographic form in the notorious "trollface" JPEG, developed by the Oakland artist Carlos Ramirez in 2008, which is often posted on message boards under the phrase "U MAD BRO?" or was, in an earlier micro-period of online archives of male masochistic terror.

The internet has seemingly decided that a highly specific kind of black comedy is the only genre through which the abjection, negativity, and violence of the present can be mediated. Such a development might invite a familiar recitation of Marx's famous line about tragedy and farce, except that "farce" is not quite the right word for these comedies, if that term signifies the proliferation of multiplicities of connection, through sex, through law, and through the bathos of embodiment. The genre by which farce has been displaced is one in which there is no connection—sexual, legal, or embodied— that will come into being to surprise or (as it once did) delight. First as farce, then as dank: a fascist lawmaker jacking off a Democrat in the third row of the Denver regional performance of the *Beetlejuice* musical.

Symptomatic of the becoming-comic of the present might also be, then, the collapse of the particular form of comic seriality that I have been describing here. An awkward and belated question seems inevitable: what if the serial sitcom were not, in fact, a serial circuit but a *parallel* one? What if each *Simpsons* episode—in which, again, nobody ages, or for the most part mentions any other adventure—were not supposed to follow from the previous episode in any kind of proceeding sequence but rather to substitute for it, as though taking place in a parallel universe? What if each *Simpsons* episode presented a different thing that could happen to this family—each of the multitudinous possibilities arranged in a latitude of infinite breadth and no prospect of advancing one step further in plot? Does such a prospect feel preferable to the infinite recursion or even more disorienting and banal—more or less like the compulsion to repeat that Freud describes in "Beyond the Pleasure Principle"? This conceit structures one of the more interesting post-sitcoms of the past few years: *Rick and Morty*, an animated narrative loosely modeled after the relationship between Doc and Marty in *Back to the Future* but where time travel (a narrative problematic of the serial age) has been replaced by travel between parallel universes.

Yet the infinity of narrative possibilities—infinite Ricks and infinite Mortys but also a world in which everyone walks around with a hamster in their butt, a world where every hamster walks around with a person in their butt, and so on—shapes the kinds of stakes that the show can develop. In an early episode, Rick makes a love potion to help Morty woo a girl he likes but it mutates and then spreads virally across the globe until every person alive has been turned into monstrous fleshy creatures that Rick calls "Cronenbergs," incapable

E.3 Rick and Morty stand in front of the council of Ricks in a yellow room in *Rick and Morty*.

of communication or rational thought. Rather than, as the viewer expects, using an antidote to neutralize plot and reestablish situation, Rick and Morty simply identify another universe, in which some *other* Rick successfully solved the Cronenberg problem *and* both have died in an unrelated explosion seconds afterward. The Rick and Morty from the now-abandoned original universe then bury the bodies of their indigenous counterparts in the back yard and take their place, as if nothing had ever happened. While we see Morty shaken by the ordeal, we also recognize that his distress derives from a redundant attachment not merely to a social setting—everyone he has ever known has been monstrously transformed—but more fundamentally to a progressive, linear temporality out of which he has been wrested and into which he will never return. To be sure, relinquishing progressive chronology can hardly be narrated without its own share of paradoxes. The trauma of having been ripped from his initial timeline stays with Morty, and he carries it within himself, a singular timeline distinct from that of any other character, presuming, as we are generally supposed to do, that Rick has done everything many times before—that, indeed, his best adventures took place years ago, and we're watching something like his flop era.

Two episodes later, the parallel universe problem engulfs Rick and Morty's whole family as they gain access to "interdimensional goggles," which allow them to see through the eyes of their inter-dimensional counterparts. After finding worlds in which Morty's parents, Jerry and Beth, terminated their first pregnancy and separated, the group grows increasingly convinced that they would all be happier if they hadn't formed a family. Morty's sister Summer, dismayed by her parents' dismay, packs a backpack and prepares to depart, telling her brother, "You're not the cause of your parents' misery. You're just a symptom of it." Declining to abandon Summer to complete nonrelation, Morty tells her about the events of Cronenberg world and gestures to the graves he and Rick dug for their counterparts. He admits then that he's not her brother but adds, "I'm better than your brother. I'm a version of your brother you can trust when he says, 'Don't run.' Nobody exists on purpose. Nobody belongs anywhere. Everybody's gonna die. Come watch TV?" He has become blackpilled: having reconciled himself to the essential meaningless of the world, he turns to television—which is *also* interdimensional and therefore incomprehensibly surreal—to farm his own lolz.

What would it mean to relinquish the diagnostic implications of "binge watching"? What would it mean to relinquish the productivity-shaming language of "procrastination"? Is there a therapeutics of the sitcom—failing that, a propaedeutics? The sit-com, after all, habituates itself to a present without promising a future correction, or a final diagnosis, by which our sicknesses can be treated and we can be shuffled back into the capitalist work relation that promises to supply Americans, no less than Communists, an eschatological plotline. Marx distrusted such workers as had been stripped of plot, the *lumpen*—perhaps, that is to say, the *lumpy*, but perhaps also the *lump*, the rogue. The procrasturbating sitcom binger might be, on some level, *depressed*, but she might also be "passively rotting mass thrown off by the lowest layers of old society," a cultural bottom feeder.[8] Her knowledge is outdated and probably unmonetizable; her desires dislocate her from the erotic and legal plots of personhood, unlike those of the rom-com junkie, whose hope of finding *the one* keeps her showing up to the office, keeps her buying Kinder eggs. The reassuring fantasy that her depression "is political" never cuts into the eternally extensive present, never accelerates her commitments, never quickens her pulse. *Of course* it's fucking political. *Everything*'s political. But genre does something that "the political" can't, or won't, and that's better than nothing.

NOTES

Formula

1   Stelter, "Ownership of TV Sets Falls in U.S."
2   TVtropes.org, "Egg Sitting," https://tvtropes.org/pmwiki/pmwiki.php
    /Main/EggSitting.
3   Jeffreys, *Unpacking Queer Politics*, 19.
4   Ngai, *Our Aesthetic Categories*.

Part One. Full House

1   Spigel, *Make Room for TV*, 10.
2   Freud, "Femininity," 356.
3   Lacan, "Seminar 15," 9.
4   Bersani, "Is the Rectum a Grave?"
5   Bersani, "Is There a Gay Art?," 33.
6   Allen, "Lesbian Economics," 163.
7   Berlant and Warner, "Sex in Public," 547.
8   White, *Uninvited*.
9   Fabian, *Time and the Other*, xxvii.
10 "Loving v. Virginia," last updated December 14, 2022, https://www
    .history.com/topics/black-history/loving-v-virginia.
11 Loving v. Virginia, 388 US 1 (1967).
12 UK Local Government Act 1988, section 28, https://www.legislation.gov
    .uk/ukpga/1988/9/section/28/enacted.
13 Ely, *The Adventures of Amos 'n' Andy*, 105, 174–75. See also "What the
    People Think!" and "Amos 'n' Andy."
14 On the efforts to move the show from radio to TV, see Hawes, *Filmed
    Television Drama, 1952–1958*, 72.

15 "Amos 'n' Andy Pick TV Successors," 21.

16 "Amos 'n' Andy Call It Quits," 18.

17 "Amos 'n' Andy Creators Plan New TV Show," 61.

18 Du Bois, "Bound by the Color Line."

19 "Jerry Mathers Interview Part 3," YouTube, 2011, https://www.youtube.com/watch?v=6eYr8KSByvk.

20 *Urban Dictionary*, s.v. "Tweeter" and "Beaver," accessed September 18, 2023, https://www.urbandictionary.com/define.php?term=beaver and https://www.urbandictionary.com/define.php?term=tweeter.

21 Bateson, *Steps to an Ecology of Mind*.

22 Laing and Esterson, *Sanity, Madness and the Family*.

23 "(2004) Bill Cosby, 'The Pound Cake Speech,'" BlackPast, https://www.blackpast.org/african-american-history/2004-bill-cosby-pound-cake-speech/.

24 Assembly Bill 489, California Legislature, 1975–1976 Regular Session.

25 Levin, "Compton's Cafeteria Riot."

26 Sondheim, *Company*.

Part Two. Friends

1 Anderson, "O Superman (For Massnet)."

2 Laozi, *Tao Te Ching*, chapter 38.

3 Mao, "On Contradiction."

4 Greene, "Meat Loaf Remembers Jim Steinman."

5 Freud, "The Theme of the Three Caskets," 292.

6 Freud, "The Theme of the Three Caskets," 301.

7 Freud, "The Theme of the Three Caskets," 301.

8 Marx and Engels, *The German Ideology*, 53.

9 Freud, "Three Essays on the Theory of Sexuality."

10 Freud, "Three Essays on the Theory of Sexuality."

11 Kelsey-Sugg, "How We Fell in and out of Love with the Laff Box."

12 Markbreiter, "'Other Trans People Make Me Dysphoric.'"

13 Friend, "First Banana."

14 Lee, "Richard Pryor, Now Your Ex-Wife Is Calling."

15 For this insight, which they are developing into a brilliant and expansive reading of depictions of chemistry in the age of offshored chemical manufacturing, I am grateful to my dear friend Mat Paskins.

16 *Horsin' Around*, Netflix (2014).

17 Ghert-Zand, "Comedy Writer Gallops to Success with 'BoJack Horseman.'"

18 Spigel, *Make Room for TV*.

19   Stephen Eldridge, "Chekhov's Gun," *Encyclopedia Britannica*, accessed
      March 17, 2002, https://www.britannica.com/topic/Chekhovs-gun.
20   Hemingway, "The Art of the Short Story."

Epilogue. Parallels

1   Seltzer, *Serial Killers*.
2   Berlant, "On the Case," 663.
3   Foucault, "The Order of the Discourse," 69.
4   Villiers de L'Isle-Adam, *Claire Lenoir*, 220.
5   Gutkin, "The Dandified Dick," 1299.
6   See Mulvey, "Visual Pleasure and Narrative Cinema"; and Ahmed,
      Feminist Killjoy Handbook.
7   Groves and Gomez Licon, "'Day by Day.'"
8   Marx and Engels, *The Manifesto of the Communist Party*, 29.

WORKS CITED

Television and Film

The Addams Family. Created by David Levy. "The Addams Family Goes to School." Season 1, episode 1. Filmways, Inc., 1964.

Amos 'n' Andy. Created by Charles Correll and Freeman Gosden. CBS Television, 1951–53.

Arrested Development. Created by Mitch Hurwitz. "Altar Egos." Season 1, episode 16. Image Television, The Hurwitz Company, and 20th Century Fox Television, 2004.

Arrested Development. Created by Mitch Hurwitz. "Exit Strategy." Season 3, episode 12. Image Television, The Hurwitz Company, and 20th Century Fox Television, 2006.

Arrested Development. Created by Mitch Hurwitz. "Let 'Em Eat Cake." Season 1, episode 22. Image Television, The Hurwitz Company, and 20th Century Fox Television, 2004.

Bill and Ted's Excellent Adventure. Directed by Stephen Herek. Interscope Communications and Nelson Entertainment, 1989. 1 hour, 30 minutes.

Blue Velvet. Directed by David Lynch. De Laurentiis Entertainment Group, 1986. 2 hours.

Bob's Burgers. Created by Loren Bouchard. Wilo Productions, 2011–present.

BoJack Horseman. Created by Raphael Bob-Waksberg. "Escape from L.A." Season 2, episode 11. Netflix, 2015.

Boy Meets World. Created by Michael Jacobs and April Kelly. "Cult Fiction." Season 4, episode 21. Buena Vista Television, 1997.

The Brady Bunch. Created by Sherwood Schwartz. CBS Television, 1969–74.

Breaking Bad. Created by Vince Gilligan. Sony Pictures Television, 2008–13.

Brooklyn Nine-Nine. Created by Dan Goor and Michael Schur. NBCUniversal Television, 2013–21.

Community. Created by Dan Harmon. "Competitive Wine Tasting." Season 2, episode 20. Sony Pictures Television, 2011.

The Cosby Show. Created by Bill Cosby. "Theo and the Joint." Season 1, episode 17. Carsey-Werner Productions, 1985.

The Dick Van Dyke Show. Created by Carl Reiner. "It May Look Like a Walnut." Season 2, episode 20. Calvada Productions, 1963.

Diff'rent Strokes. Created by Jeff Harris and Bernie Kukoff. "Sam's Missing." Season 8, episode 1. Embassy Telecommunications, 1985.

Everybody Hates Chris. Created by Chris Rock and Ali LeRoi. "Everybody Hates Eggs." Season 2, episode 11. CBS Television, 2007.

Family Guy. Created by Seth MacFarlane. 20th Century Fox Television, 1999–present.

Family Matters. Created by William Bickley and Michael Warren. "Dr. Urkel and Mr. Cool." Season 5, episode 8. Warner Bros., 1993.

Family Matters. Created by William Bickley and Michael Warren. "Laura's First Date." Season 1, episode 12. Warner Bros., 1989.

Family Ties. Created by Gary David Goldberg. Paramount Domestic Television, 1982–89.

Frasier. Created by David Angell, Peter Casey, and David Lee. "Flour Child." Season 2, episode 4. Paramount Global Content, 1994.

Fresh Off the Boat. Created by Nahnatchka Khan. 20th Century Fox Television, 2015–20.

The Fresh Prince of Bel-Air. Created by Andy Borowitz and Susan Borowitz. Warner Bros. Television, 1990–96.

Friends. Created by David Crane and Marta Kauffman. "The Last One—Part II." Season 10, episode 18. Warner Bros., 2004.

Friends. Created by David Crane and Marta Kauffman. "The One with the Prom Video." Season 2, episode 14. Warner Bros., 1996.

Full House. Created by Jeff Franklin. "Shape Up." Season 4, episode 8. Warner Bros. Television, 1990.

Happy Days. Created by Garry Marshall. "My Favorite Orkan." Season 5, episode 22. CBS Television, 1978.

A Hard Day's Night. Directed by Richard Lester. Criterion Collection, 1964. 87 minutes.

Head. Directed by Bob Rafelson. Columbia Pictures, 1968. 86 minutes.

Hollywood Squares. Created by Merrill Heatter and Bob Quigley. Heatter-Quigley Productions, 1966–80.

Home Improvement. Created by Carmen Finestra, David McFadzean, and Matt Williams. "Pilot." Season 1, episode 1. Buena Vista Television, 1991.

House, M.D. Created by David Shore. "Don't Ever Change." Season 4, episode 12. NBCUniversal, 2008.

House, M.D. Created by David Shore. "House's Head." Season 4, episode 15. NBCUniversal, 2008.

House, M.D. Created by David Shore. "Wilson's Heart." Season 4, episode 16. NBCUniversal, 2008.

How I Met Your Mother. Created by Carter Bays and Craig Thomas. 20th Century Fox Television, 2005–14.

I Love Lucy. Produced by Desi Arnaz. Desilu Productions, 1951–57.

I'm Alan Partridge. Created by Peter Baynham, Steve Coogan, and Armando Iannucci. BBC Two, 1997–2002.

King of the Hill. Created by Mike Judge and Greg Daniels. 20th Century Fox Television, 1997–2009.

The Larry Sanders Show. Created by Garry Shandling and Dennis Klein. HBO Entertainment, 1992–98.

Leave It to Beaver. Created by Joe Connelly and Bob Mosher. "Family Scrapbook." Season 6, episode 39. MCA TV, 1963.

Leave It to Beaver. Created by Joe Connelly and Bob Mosher. "The Pipe." Season 2, episode 9. MCA TV, 1958.

Lilo & Stitch. Directed by Chris Sanders and Dean DeBlois. Walt Disney Pictures, 2002.

Mad About You. Created by Paul Reiser and Danny Jacobson. Columbia Pictures and Columbia TriStar, 1992–99.

Married . . . with Children. Created by Michael G. Moye and Ron Leavitt. Sony Pictures Television, 1987–97.

The Mary Tyler Moore Show. Created by James L. Brooks and Allan Burns. "Love Is All Around." Season 1, episode 1. MTM Enterprises, 1970.

The Mindy Project. Created by Mindy Kaling. NBCUniversal Television, 2012–17.

Modern Family. Created by Christopher Lloyd and Steven Levitan. "Pilot." Season 1, episode 1. 20th Century Fox Television, 2009.

The Monkees. Created by Bob Rafelson and Bert Schneider. Sony Pictures Television, 1966–68.

Mork and Mindy. Created by Garry Marshall, Dale McRaven, and Joe Glauberg. CBS Television, 1978–82.

The Munsters. Created by Allan Burns and Chris Haywood. NBCUniversal Television, 1964–66.

My Favorite Martian. Created by John L. Greene. Jack Chertok Television in association with CBS, 1963–66.

My Favorite Martians. Directed by Hal Sutherland. CBS, 1973–75.

New Girl. Created by Elizabeth Meriwether. "Pilot." Season 1, episode 1. 20th Century Fox Television, 2011.

The New Leave It to Beaver. Created by Brian Levant. Telvan Productions, 1983–89.

The New Normal. Created by Ryan Murphy and Ali Adler. 20th Century Fox Television, 2012–13.

The Office. Created by Greg Daniels. "The Fight." Season 2, episode 6. NBCUniversal, 2005.

The Office. Created by Greg Daniels. "Goodbye, Michael." Season 7, episode 22. NBCUniversal, 2011.

The Office. Created by Greg Daniels. "New Boss." Season 5, episode 20. NBCUniversal, 2009.

Old Baby. Written by Maria Bamford. Netflix, 2017.

Phyllis. Created by James L. Brooks, Stan Daniels, and Ed. Weinberger. MTM Enterprises, 1975–77.

A Place to Stand. Directed by Christopher Chapman. Ontario Department of Economics and Development, 1967. 17 minutes.

Pushing Daisies. Created by Bryan Fuller. Warner Bros. Television, 2007–9.

Rhoda. Created by James L. Brooks and Allan Burns. "Two Little Words . . . Marriage Counselor." Season 3, episode 6. MTM Enterprises, 1976.

Rick and Morty. Created by Justin Roiland and Dan Harmon. "Rick Potion #9." Season 1, episode 6. Warner Bros. Television, 2014.

Rick and Morty. Created by Justin Roiland and Dan Harmon. "Rixty Minutes." Season 1, episode 8. Warner Bros. Television, 2014.

The Royal Tenenbaums. Directed by Wes Anderson. Buena Vista Pictures, 2001.

The Simpsons. Created by Matt Groening. 20th Century Fox Television, 1989–present.

Sister, Sister. Created by Kim Bass, Gary Gilbert, and Fred Shafferman. "Scrambled Eggs." Season 2. episode 15. Paramount Domestic Television, 1995.

Sitcom. Directed by François Ozon. Mars Distribution, 1998. 85 minutes.

South Park. Created by Trey Parker and Matt Stone. "Cartman Gets an Anal Probe." Season 1, episode 1. Paramount Global, 1997.

The Spoils of Babylon. Created by Matt Piedmont and Andrew Steele. "The Rise of Empire." Season 1, episode 4. Funny or Die, 2014.

Still the Beaver. Directed by Steven Hilliard Stern. CBS, 1983. 120 minutes.

Stranger Things. Created by the Duffer Brothers. Netflix, 2016–present.

That '70s Show. Created by Bonnie Turner, Terry Turner, and Mark Brazil. "The Trials of Michael Kelso." Season 3, episode 18. Carsey-Werner Productions, 2001.

Third Rock from the Sun. Created by Bonnie Turner and Terry Turner. "Brains and Eggs." Season 1, episode 1. Carsey-Werner Company, 1996.

30 Rock. Created by Tina Fey. NBC Television, 2006–13.

The Thomas Crown Affair. Directed by Norman Jewison. United Artists, 1968. 102 minutes.

Together, Together. Directed by Nikole Beckwith. Bleecker Street, 2021. 90 minutes.

True Colors. Created by Michael Weithorn. Fox, 1990–92.

The Truman Show. Directed by Peter Weir. Paramount Pictures, 1998. 103 minutes.

Twin Peaks. Created by Mark Frost and David Lynch. "Pilot." Season 1, episode 1. CBS Television, 1990–91.

Who's the Boss? Created by Martin Cohan and Blake Hunter. "Pilot." Season 1, episode 1. Sony Pictures Television, 1984.

Literature

Ahmed, Sara. *The Feminist Killjoy Handbook*. New York: Seal Press, 2023.

Allen, Jeffner M. "Lesbian Economics." In *Queer Economics: A Reader*, edited by Joyce Jacobsen and Adam Zellner, 160–77. New York: Routledge, 2008.

"Amos 'n' Andy." *Pittsburgh Courier*, April 25, 1931.

"Amos 'n' Andy Call it Quits." Associated Press, June 10, 1951.

"Amos 'n' Andy Creators Plan New TV Show." *Jet*, March 3, 1955.

"Amos 'n' Andy Pick TV Successors." Associated Press, June 9, 1951.

Anderson, Laurie. "O Superman (For Massenet)." Written by Roma Baran and Laurie Anderson. Track 6 on *Big Science*. Warner Records, 1981.

Bateson, Gregory. *Steps to an Ecology of Mind: Collected Essays in Anthropology, Psychiatry, Evolution, and Epistemology*. San Francisco: Chandler Publishing, 1972.

Berlant, Lauren. "On the Case." *Critical Inquiry* 33, no. 4 (2007): 663–72.

Berlant, Lauren, and Michael Warner. "Sex in Public." *Critical Inquiry* 24, no. 2 (1998): 547–66.

Bersani, Leo. "Is There a Gay Art?" In *Is the Rectum a Grave? And Other Essays*, 31–36. Chicago: University of Chicago Press, 2010.

Bersani, Leo. "Is the Rectum a Grave?" In *Is the Rectum a Grave? And Other Essays*, 3–30. Chicago: University of Chicago Press, 2010.

Dahl, Melissa. *Cringeworthy: A Theory of Awkwardness*. New York: Portfolio/Penguin, 2018.

Du Bois, W. E. B. "Bound by the Color Line." *New Masses* 58, no. 7 (1946): 8.

Ely, Melvin Patrick. *The Adventures of Amos 'n' Andy*. Charlottesville: University of Virginia Press, 2001.

Fabian, Johannes. *Time and Other: How Anthropology Makes Its Object*. New York: Columbia University Press, 2014.

Faludi, Susan. *Stiffed: The Betrayal of the American Man*. New York: HarperCollins, 1999.

Foucault, Michel. "The Order of the Discourse." In *Untying the Text: A Post-structuralist Reader*, edited by Robert Young, 48–78. Boston: Routledge and Kegan Paul, 1981.

Freud, Sigmund. "Beyond the Pleasure Principle." In *The Standard Edition of the Complete Psychological Works of Sigmund Freud*, vol. 18, translated by James Strachey, 7–64. London: Hogarth, 1920.

Freud, Sigmund, "Femininity." In *Freud on Women: A Reader*, edited by Elisabeth Young-Breuel, 342–62. New York: W. W. Norton, 1990.

Freud, Sigmund. *Jokes and Their Relation to the Unconscious*. Translated by James Strachey. New York: W. W. Norton, 1905.

Freud, Sigmund. "On the Sexual Theories of Children." In *The Standard Edition of the Complete Psychological Works of Sigmund Freud*, vol. 9, translated by James Strachey, 205–26. London: Hogarth, 1908.

Freud, Sigmund. "The Theme of the Three Caskets." In *The Standard Edition of the Complete Psychological Works of Sigmund Freud*, vol. 12, translated by James Strachey, 291–301. London: Hogarth, 1913.

Freud, Sigmund. "Three Essays on the Theory of Sexuality." In *The Standard Edition of the Complete Psychological Works of Sigmund Freud*, vol. 7, translated by James Strachey, 126–43. London: Hogarth, 1905.

Friend, Tad. "First Banana." *New Yorker*, June 28, 2010.

Ghert-Zand, Renee. "Comedy Writer Gallops to Success with 'BoJack Horseman.'" *Times of Israel*, September 4, 2015.

Greene, Andy. "Meat Loaf Remembers Jim Steinman: 'He Was the Centerpiece of My Life.'" *Rolling Stone*, April 23, 2021.

Groves, Stephen, and Adriana Gomez Licon. "'Day by Day': Uvalde Survivors Recover from Wounds, Trauma." Associated Press, June 2, 2022.

Gutkin, Len. "The Dandified Dick: Hardboiled Noir and the Wildean Epigram." *ELH* 81, no. 4 (2014): 1299–1326.

Hawes, William. *Filmed Television Drama, 1952–1958*. Jefferson, NC: McFarland, 2002.

Hemingway, Ernest. "The Art of the Short Story." *Paris Review*, Spring 1981.

Jeffreys, Sheila. *Unpacking Queer Politics: A Lesbian Feminist Perspective*. Cambridge, UK: Polity, 2003.

Kelsey-Sugg, Anna. "How We Fell in and out of Love with the Laff Box, the Laugh Track Machine That Changed Sitcoms Forever." ABC Australia, April 15, 2020.

Kollontai, Alexandra. *A Great Love*. Translated by Lily Lore. New York: Vanguard Press, 1929.

Lacan, Jacques. "Seminar 15: Tuesday 11 June 1974." http://www.lacaninireland.com/web/wp-content/uploads/2010/06/THE-SEMINAR-OF-JACQUES-LACAN-XXI.pdf.

Laing, R. D. *The Politics of the Family*. Toronto: House of Anansi Press, 1993.

Laing, R. D., and Aaron Esterson. *Sanity, Madness and the Family: Families of Schizophrenics*. New York: Routledge, 2017.

Laozi. *Tao Te Ching*. Translated by Gia-fu Feng and Jane English. Accessed April 2, 2022. https://www.wussu.com/laotzu/laotzu38.html.

Lee, Jennifer. "Richard Pryor, Now Your Ex-Wife Is Calling." *People*, June 16, 1986.

Leiris, Michel. *Nights as Day, Days as Night*. Translated by Richard Sieburth. Sacramento, CA: Spurl Editions, 2017.

Levin, Sam. "Compton's Cafeteria Riot: A Historic Act of Trans Resistance, Three Years before Stonewall." *The Guardian*, June 21, 2019.

Mao Tse-tung. "On Contradiction." August 1937. https://www.marxists.org /reference/archive/mao/selected-works/volume-1/mswv1_17.htm.

Markbreiter, Charlie. "'Other Trans People Make Me Dysphoric': Trans Assimilation and Cringe." *New Inquiry*, March 1, 2022.

Marx, Karl, and Friedrich Engels. *The German Ideology*. New York: International Publishers, 1947.

Marx, Karl, and Friedrich Engels. *The Manifesto of the Communist Party*. Chicago: Charles H. Kerr, 1906.

Mulvey, Laura. "Visual Pleasure and Narrative Cinema." *Screen* 16, no. 3 (1975): 6–18.

Ngai, Sianne. *Our Aesthetic Categories: Zany, Cute, Interesting*. Cambridge, MA: Harvard University Press, 2015.

Pryor, Richard. *. . . And It's Deep Too! The Complete Warner Bros. Recordings (1968-1992)*. Warner Archives/Rhino/Atlantic Records, 2000.

Ramirez, Carlos. *Trollface*. September 19, 2008. Oakland, CA. Digital drawing.

Ronell, Avital. "Support Our Tropes: Reading Desert Storm." In *The UberReader: Selected Works of Avital Ronell*, 38–62. Champaign: University of Illinois Press, 2010.

Seltzer, Mark. *Serial Killers: Life and Death in America's Wound Culture*. New York: Routledge, 1998.

Shakespeare, William. *The Merchant of Venice*. The Yale Shakespeare. New Haven, CT: Yale University Press, 1923.

Shakespeare, William. *A Midsummer Night's Dream*. Boston: Athenaeum Press, 1910.

Sondheim, Stephen. *Company: A Musical Comedy*. New York: Random House, 1970.

Spigel, Lynn. *Make Room for TV: Television and the Family Ideal in Postwar America*. Chicago: University of Chicago Press, 1992.

Steinman, Jim. "Making Love Out of Nothing at All." Track 6 on *Greatest Hits*, by Air Supply. Arista Records, 1983.

Stelter, Brian. "Ownership of TV Sets Falls in U.S." *New York Times*, May 3, 2011.

TVtropes.org. "Egg Sitting." Accessed May 20, 2022. https://tvtropes.org
/pmwiki/pmwiki.php/Main/EggSitting.

Villiers de L'Isle-Adam, Auguste de. *Claire Lenoir*. Translated by Arthur Symons.
New York: Albert and Charles Boni, 1925.

"What the People Think!" *Pittsburgh Courier*, May 2, 1934.

White, Patricia. *Uninvited: Classical Hollywood Cinema and Lesbian Representability.*
Bloomington: Indiana University Press, 1999.

INDEX